Awaken

Your

Assertion

A journey of self-discovery
that inspires transformation
from the inside out.

Karen Davies

First Self-Published in United Kingdom by:
My Well-being, Taunton, Somerset, United Kingdom

Copyright © Karen Davies, My Well-being 2014
Edition 1

A catalogue record for this book is available from the British Library.

ISBN-13: 978-1495286247

Dedicated to all my past-participants, coaching clients, friends and family who have subtly, or directly shaped the creation of this book. With love and gratitude for all that you have helped me become.

Contents

About the Author

There is a growing realisation that to thrive in today's crazy world there are a new set of rules to play by to maintain our sanity. As a result, we get thrown into chaos and an existence that expects us to juggle family, career and friends, whilst trying to make time for us – not an easy task.

Developing assertiveness is one sure way of working through these challenges. Yet to make a real difference, we must go beyond learning the standard *assertive norms* – we need a far more profound journey to achieve a meaningful and long-lasting change.

A web of thoughts, feelings, beliefs and behaviours binds our assertiveness and when we unravel its intricacies and discover the world that is 'planet me', we can achieve greater fulfilment. With a positive mind, healthy behaviours and new philosophies, we can flourish and say goodbye to stress and hello to well-being.

Whatever walk of life you come to this book from, you will gain so many benefits, delving into its pages of inspiration. If you need to enhance your effectiveness, make more time for yourself, reduce stress, improve health and relationships, then investing in this development journey will prove so valuable to you.

I am passionate about my work in developing the art of authentic assertion and confidence. Whilst I have been in the personal development and coaching fields for twenty-five years, it has been in the last fifteen that my work has had the greatest impact, thanks to my own self-discovery. After suffering from stress-related depression in 1997, I had the chance to explore myself profoundly and uncover what was behind my health crisis. After a soul-searching self-development process, I worked through my challenges and these have become the source of my healing, my inspirational teachings and my powerful coaching.

With my self-employment hat on, I have inspired changes in many executives, leaders and aspiring team players across the globe, achieving success in my personal development arena for fifteen years.

Although more recently I have been inspired to practise what I preach - so have said goodbye to my corporate life and am now putting all my energy into helping create personal transformation, inspiring the fulfilment of individuals, through my new vocation – Conversations with a Butterfly.

My approach to personal development is so far beyond the concept of the traditional 'training course'. I use my coaching philosophy to guide people on a path of self-discovery, building on the notion that teaching is a passive activity; learning is active. You will not just read this book, you will be inspired to take a journey and, engaged by my coaching exercises, have the opportunity to alter the way you think, how you feel and behave in areas of your life.

Your transformation is just around the corner.

Karen Davies, Conversations with a Butterfly

www.conversationswithabutterfly.com
www.facebook.com/mywellbeinguk

<u>Part 1</u>

Getting to Know the Real You

Chapter 1 - Introduction
A New Perspective

"A journey of a thousand miles begins with a single step."

Laozi, Chinese Philosopher

How many times have you read a self-help book or article with the intention to change? After a month, or may be only a few weeks, you realise that, inadvertently, your old habits have returned to haunt you. Does this sound familiar?

I have seen this all too often and call this the *sticking plaster* effect. We try to solve a problem with a quick-fix approach, hoping it goes away. Yet, when we remove the plaster, we reopen the wound. Until we get beneath why the problem exists in the first place, we will never achieve a meaningful change.

Assertive development has historically focused on providing strategies that *should* achieve better results when applied with honest commitment. So why then, when we have the desire to change do we still feel stuck and frustrated?

I believe there is a missing piece to the assertive jigsaw; a gap that allows our old patterns to return. That gap is the fundamentals of *reflection* and *self-understanding*.

Author Stephen Covey's inside-out philosophy inspires my approach to personal growth and I believe, before we can improve relationships, interact more positively or say 'no' confidently, we must first look within. We must be prepared to look at what influences us to behave unassertively, consider what holds us back and check out the quality of our inner-confidence. These all-important nuggets of information provide amazing insights into the triggers that shape how we habitually think and feel and the driving force behind our behaviours. Only then can we move forward.

Without this *inside-out* approach, it is like trying to knit a jumper from a tangled ball of wool. It is a virtually impossible task until it is unravelled. If we want more success and happiness, we can no longer rely on the *sticking plaster*. We need the courage to look inside and unravel the intricate web that makes us who we are.

We can then make the profound changes that give us the basis for long-lasting change. This may feel scary; may-be it is exciting; either way it will be an adventure and one that I invite you to embark upon with me as your guide.

As author Susan Jeffers says,

"Feel the fear and do it anyway."

Why Develop Assertiveness?

When you look back at the people in your life who have positively influenced you, what is it about them that stand out? Is it their intimidation, their power, their ability to shout above others or their ruthlessness? Perhaps it is their submissiveness, shyness, how they follow others or their willingness to work late regularly.

I suspect it is more likely their compassion, their fairness, their ability to listen, support and negotiate and their unerring strength to stand up for themselves. How often do we find ourselves wishing to be more like them?

Demands on our energy and time come from all avenues; from friends, family, work and add to that all the pressure of job security and general health and well-being. These have a direct and indirect impact on how we behave, often resulting in internal conflicts, anxiety and stress.

It would be easy for us to try to meet everyone's needs, although I believe this causes real stress, which ultimately affects our health. According to a recent survey by *UK's Health and Safety Executive*, self-reported stress and depression accounts for 12.8 million lost workdays per year. So there has to be a better way – there is – the path is authentic assertion. No more wishing we could be like others; no more being driven by external demands. Instead, we could generate a future of happiness and fulfilment, which is inspired by honouring ourselves and treating others fairly.

The Assertive Way – The Power of Three

Welcome to the book that helps us along a transformational journey of self-discovery, where we can reflect on our internal map of the world, explore our values and understand how these have shaped the way we think, feel and react today.

Over the last twenty-five years, I have run nearly one hundred Assertiveness, Leadership and Personal Development Workshops and my experiences and the participants who have graced me with their

10

presence on these sessions have all influenced me to write this book. With such a huge and powerfully thought-provoking topic, I felt that it justified being broken down into three essential ingredients, hence the three significant sections, all wrapped up in one book.

My thinking is that each section needs time, reflection and practise and so with the three parts, it encourages us to take time, in between each section, to stop and take stock of our learning, before moving forward.

Here are the three powerful sections that make up this book:

Part 1 – Getting to Know the Real You

The first section helps us look inwards and, through our increased awareness, understand what is stopping us from being more assertive. By the end of this section, we will understand the modern truth about our behaviour and have seven powerful thinking and behaving strategies to develop our assertion. With this knowledge and those strategies, we will be compelled to take inspiring action.

Part 2 – Creating Unshakeable Self-esteem

Part 2 illustrates the role our internal and external interactions have on our confidence and assertion. We examine the evolving science behind the brain, allowing us to explore the quality of our self-esteem and the impact that our inner beliefs have on our world. I offer a process for eliminating our self-destructive mental programmes, making way for an authentic confidence and an unshakeable self-esteem.

In addition, we leave Part 2 with the tools for clear and concise communication that creates influential and meaningful interactions, allowing us to say what we need in a positive, empathic and confident way.

Part 3 – Assertive Strategy Guide

This final part of this book gives us the last dose of magic - *situational assertion strategies*. Selected from real-life events that past-participants have shared and have agreed I can use, we cover specific assertive techniques that help deal with particularly difficult experiences or behaviour 'types', arming us with practical tips and guidance. This creates an assertive toolbox we can access at any time to handle a range of diverse situations more effectively.

The result will be a more self-assured person who can build solid relationships and stand up for themselves more confidently; we will walk differently, talk differently and feel differently.

What to Expect from this Book

I have written this in the style of a workbook that encourages us to interact and to engage with the material. As a personal coach, we will explore what being assertive means in our life-context and help develop a personal jigsaw that pieces together a picture of powerful insights and self-knowledge, enabling us to review our effectiveness. It will be like having a personal guide.

Our journey together will provide solutions to our challenges; enabling us to make conscious choices and build an authentic inner confidence that serves all areas of our lives.

There will be exercises encouraging us to reflect and journalise, indicated throughout the book by this hand symbol and I encourage taking time out to think profoundly around questions that I pose, as they will ultimately help make a more meaningful change.

If you are ready, let's take the first step.

"The beginning is the most important part of the work."

Plato

Chapter 2 – Assertive Clarity

"Would you tell me please which way I ought to go from here? That depends a good deal, on where you want to get to."

Alice in Wonderland – Lewis Carol

Before uncovering some assertive myths, I would like you to think about why you have chosen to read this book and what you hope to learn. Please answer the following questions to get clarity about what assertive development means to you:

Personal Goals and Expectations

1. Create a vision of what you imagine yourself looking, sounding and feeling like, in say a year's time or six months perhaps, having read this book. List what would be different for you.

2. Think about what it is that you think stops you from behaving assertively, right now, and in particular, what type of situations challenge you the most or make you feel most anxious or stressed.

3. Given the above two questions, what do you most want to learn about your assertion and what benefits do you imagine these changes will bring you both professionally and personally?

Ok, with hopes and expectations clearly expressed, notice how we have already taken our first important assertive step. Assertion is about confidently expressing what we need or want from a person or situation and so, inadvertently, we have already practised a core assertive value. Let's move onto exploring what assertive really means.

What is Assertiveness?

Assertiveness is one of four behaviours that we show through our actions, body language and facial expressions; the other three are passive, aggressive and passive-aggressive. Each one is an external projection of our thoughts and emotions that provide the basis for our interactions. Therefore, the quality of our relationships and a situation's outcome depends upon the behaviour we display.

Here is a question to ponder:

Are we born assertive?

My belief is that we are **not** born assertive, it is a learned behaviour and here is why I believe that.

Think about an animal born in the wild; one of their early instincts is to stand and walk. These innate reflexes enable them to either *run from danger* or *stand up to fight*. Their mother does not teach these skills; they are primal, biological impulses that ensure the newborn's survival. As humans, we are powered by that same biological notion.

Bruce Lipton in his book, *The Biology of Belief* says,

"Instincts are built-in behaviours that are fundamental to the survival of all humans, independent of what culture they belong to or what time in human history they were born."

We call these instinctive behaviours:

Fight and Flight

This term was first coined by American physiologist Walter Cannon in the 1920's, summarising the theory as a complex chain of chemical reactions within the body that mobilise us to deal with danger. Those chemicals and hormones react in such a way that energy moves from our brain, liver and kidneys towards our heart, lungs and muscles to prepare us for action.

Have you ever noticed when you have faced danger that your mind blanks, rational thought disappears and your body just seems to move automatically? This is not a logical reaction; it is a natural instinct we are born with.

In today's language, *fight and flight* translates as **aggressive** and **passive** – and these primal behaviours ensure our survival.

Born with both instincts, we learn from our parents or guardians, situations and our environment, which very quickly form our conditioning, beliefs and patterns. The result is that we subconsciously develop a default for either aggression or passivity and although we use both, we generally err towards one or the other as a predominant pattern.

This default remains with us throughout life, and whilst we learn new techniques, we still gravitate towards our primal, instinctive pattern. It's not until adulthood that our brain develops a more sophisticated way of thinking and an alternative, more appropriate behaviour becomes apparent, offering better quality interactions and solutions. Yet, we find that under stress, we tend to revert to that default, although with practise we can eliminate its primal impact through assertive development.

Author Peter Honey says,

"All the other, more sophisticated behaviours develop through a process of learning and are thus more 'made' than 'born'."

What is the Moral of the Story?

I believe that we are born with a genetic make-up and a set of instinctive, primal behaviours, one of which becomes a preference that we use throughout our lives. Assertion, as a more sophisticated behaviour, we learn and through practise and repetition can be adopted as a more dominant pattern.

Assertive Myths and Irrational Beliefs

Now we understand that fight and fight are primal reactions and we can learn assertiveness, we are ready to remove some old myths and irrational beliefs that have formed around assertive behaviour.

- **I can't change the habits of a lifetime.** Not true. Whilst our behaviour patterns are habitual, they are the easiest characteristic we can change, through repetition. It therefore becomes more about *a desire to change* rather than the *possibility of changing.*

- **Assertiveness is just for women and weak men.** Wrong again. Everyone has the right and opportunity to learn a more confident, natural, fair and effective style. Assertive development is a highly inclusive topic, even for those who already consider themselves assertive.

- **Assertiveness is shouting just a little bit louder than others.** This is an often-held misconception although we don't need to raise our voices to be heard. There's a great quote that is at the heart of being assertive, which says,

'Don't raise your voice, improve your argument.'

- **People will think I've become selfish, bossy and rude.** Again, not true. When we learn the basis of assertion, we realise it isn't about being pushy. It is about keeping calm, stating confidently how we feel and interacting clearly and honestly. Assertive behaviour recognises that we have the right to ask for what we need - that is not bossy or rude.

- **I will lose sight of who I really am.** Interestingly, assertive development allows us to become *more* of who we are – the authentic us. All too often, our default behaviours become masks that protect us and that we can hide behind. Yet assertion allows the true person to emerge, through the art of honesty, self-expression and confidence.

- **Women lose their femininity when they assert themselves.** This is a very out-of-date view, as women have as much right to ask for what they need, why should that result in a loss of femininity? An assertive approach often results in greater respect, as women banish their primal defaults creating greater admiration amongst their family, friends and colleagues.

- **I shouldn't have to say what I need: people close to me should know.** Not true. Despite our best endeavours, we are not telepathic and we must learn to express what we need in order to achieve our goals. When we leave it to guesswork, we limit our success.

Behavioural Differences

Before we leave this chapter, I want to clarify what *assertiveness is and is not*. The myths listed here show that some irrational beliefs exist and yet in my experience, I believe that assertiveness has now evolved into something more inclusive, constructive and insightful. To give us a strong basis on which to understand the true nature of the different behaviour types, let's consider how we would define assertion.

Assertive Definition - Exercise

How would you **define assertive behaviour** and what specific verbal, vocal and non-verbal characteristics would you use to describe it?

Of the people you know, who are **aggressive and passive?** What do you notice about their actions, their language and the way they interact?

Behavioural Differences – A Summary

A common definition of assertion is '*being able to express our wants and needs without violating the wants and needs of others.*'

Using that assumption, here is a summary that defines all four behaviours in the Assertive Spectrum. This helps us differentiate between the four styles and carry out an initial assessment of which box best represents our predominant pattern.

Assertive	Aggressive
Assertion focuses on natural, calm and rational interactions, adopting a *win-win* philosophy. It operates from choice, measured responses and consideration of others. An assertor's own needs are honoured, yet not at the expense of others, resulting in constructive two-way interactions.	Aggression focuses on a dominant *win-lose* position. Low self-esteem and insecurity trigger this behaviour and it is used as a way of gaining power in order to feel more secure. Aggressors use force, volume and emotion to express themselves and they invest in securing their own needs above the needs of others.
With high self-esteem, assertors feel secure, listen actively and express themselves clearly. Driven by choice, they may temporarily use aggression or passivity, whilst recognising the need to return to assertion as their predominant pattern.	Aggressors command, demand and defend when threatened. Their primal reaction can result in a passive swing, as they often feel guilty about their actions, fearing rejection and consequently feel even more insecure.
Passive	**Passive Aggressive**
Passivity operates from a *people-pleasing, lose-win* position. They invest in satisfying other people's needs, at their own expense. With low self-esteem, passive style is insecure and strives to gain approval and affection. Their behaviour focuses on compliance and dependency to create security.	Passive Aggressive also operates from a *win-lose* position, although it is more indirect. Passive aggressors hide behind masks and have hidden agendas.
They rarely express themselves honestly for fear of rejection or ridicule. They project timid, shy and quietly spoken interactions where fear, anxiety and worry are key triggers for their behaviour.	Insecurity is at the heart of this behaviour, with a fear of speaking truthfully in case it offends. Yet they can do as much damage, just with less power than the pure aggressor. A need for security and self-protection dominates this behaviour, although they invest in a more subtle and indirect expression of their needs.

Self-assessment Questionnaire – An Introduction

Understanding how we come across and judging the right behaviours to use for a given situation requires a high level of self-awareness. This does not mean we have to be a chameleon. It is about considering the outcome we need, recognising that each situation or person may require a different approach and adapting our style appropriately to achieve a constructive outcome. For example, we are likely to handle a friend we've known for years differently to someone we need to interact with in a retail shop when returning an item for a refund.

The following questionnaire guides us to learn more about our behaviour patterns, how much assertion we already demonstrate and where we need to focus our development energies. There are a small number of questions to answer so the result is not necessarily conclusive, although it will indicate preferences, which lends itself to further self-study.

Work through the questions, answering them as honestly as you can. Get your journal ready so you can assess the results.

Avoid giving answers you think are the 'right' ones; answer honestly, based on how you believe you currently behave, as this will improve the assessment's accuracy.

Self-assessment Questionnaire - Instructions

Read each set of five questions carefully, assigning a number to each box using the 1-4 scale indicated at the top of the questionnaire on the next page.

Add up your scores and write the number in the Total box. We will examine what the scores mean a little later.

Always true for me	Often true	Rarely true	Never true
4	**3**	**2**	**1**

1. I appreciate people's views, even if they differ to mine. ☐

2. I listen; people find me approachable and easy to talk to. ☐

3. I ask for help easily, without feeling anxious or guilty. ☐

4. I express my feelings and opinions constructively. ☐

5. I think about my responses and their consequences. ☐

   Assertive Total ☐

6. If others are rude to me, I am rude or sarcastic back. ☐

7. I am uncomfortable letting go of tasks. ☐

8. If I disagree with someone, I always stick to my guns. ☐

9. I consider myself hot headed and easily aggravated. ☐

10. Under stress, I get short and snappy with people. ☐

   Aggressive Total ☐

11. I avoid confrontation by trying to keep the peace.

12. I hate holding eye contact as it feels like I'm staring.

13. I work hard to meet people's needs, often at my expense.

14. When asked to do something, I say 'yes' to please them.

15. Amongst authority, I feel intimidated and flustered.

   Passive Total

16. If I want someone to do a job, I butter them up first.

17. If someone upsets me, I get my own back, subtly.

18. I like to control others by behind-the-scene manoeuvres.

19. I use humour and sarcasm to handle difficult situations.

20. If I dislike someone, I subtly exclude them from events.

   Passive Aggressive Total

Now look at the next page to analyse your scores.

Self-assessment Questionnaire – Understanding your Scores

You can now interpret your scores using the following information:

- The **highest** of your four **totals** indicates that this may be your predominant behaviour.

- If that highest score is **15-20**, this may indicate a strong preference for that behaviour.

- The **lowest** of all your **totals** indicates that this may be your least preferred pattern of behaviour.

- If that lowest score is **10 or below,** may indicate how infrequently, you use this behaviour.

- If all your **totals** are low, this may indicate an overall level of passivity, showing a lack of self-belief and doubt in your ability when answering the questions.

- If **assertive and passive totals are close**, this may indicate a strengthening of your assertive approach. It shows you are asserting yourself more often, although a predominant passive insecurity influences a retreat to a people-pleasing position.

- If **passive and aggressive totals are close**, this may indicate a low self-esteem and insecurity, which underlies both behaviours. You may, for example, bottle up emotions and then explode with frustration. You then feel guilty about your outburst and return to a passive standpoint.

- If **assertive and aggressive totals are close**, this may indicate an imbalance of your self-expression and a dominant feeling of frustration. As you experiment with your assertion, you may still find yourself shouting or finger pointing when you struggle to get your views across. This will rebalance the more you practise.

- Return to the **three non-assertive question sets** and review your **3 and 4 scores**. Think about and journalise the reasons behind your scores to those specific questions.

- Return to the **assertive question set** and review your **1 and 2 scores**. Explore what stops you from scoring higher in this area and journalise your thoughts.

- Return to your **assertive questions** and review your **3 and 4 scores**. Acknowledge the situations where you already behave assertively and explore what gives you the confidence to behave this way.

Self-assessment Summary and Exercise

The questionnaire helps you build a better understanding of your behaviour patterns and so before we move on to Chapter 3, it would be useful to build on what you've discovered.

1.   Based on the questionnaire exercise, test out your results over the next week. Form a clearer picture of your patterns by talking to people you trust about how they see you; notice your behaviours in action and take note of the habits that are most dominant for you.

2. Explore whether these behaviour patterns change in different circumstances, such as at home versus work. If they are different, explore why that might be and what is it about one part of your life that produces a more confident behaviour than the other?

3. Notice specific situations or people that influence you to react in an unassertive way. What is it about the person or event that provokes that reaction?

This brings us to the end of Chapter 2. The profound self-discovery comes in the next chapter, helping us to explore what is behind our patterns and helps us to make sense of the emerging picture.

"Our greatest enemies, the ones we must fight most often, are within." Thomas Paine

Chapter 3
Why We Do What We Do

"Better; that can be a tricky thing to find. It's only when you are curious enough to discover something new, that you can find something better."

Honda advertisement – February 2013

The last two chapters have built up a picture about assertiveness and what this means to us. This next chapter intends to pique our curiosity and help us make connections about how past influences have shaped our current behaviour. These insights have proved invaluable to past-participants and produced genuine 'light-bulb' moments, enabling them to move forward with strength and acceptance.

I recall one lady who reviewed her family's influence; she had five elder brothers. Understanding her family position and its dynamic helped her realise why she had developed a primal, 'fight' behaviour. Driven by survival and a need to earn her siblings' respect, she found herself developing an overt personality, a loud and commanding voice and, as seen by her work colleagues, a real dominant and competitive character. Once she realised it was her family environment that shaped her behaviour and that this did not make her a 'bad person', she felt released from her self-doubt, allowing her the freedom to change.

Observation Skills Exercise

For a moment, take note of what is around you or outside your nearest window. Notice the people, the objects and the noises. Observe the colours, tones, sounds and textures. How often do you observe these details and events?

How we Experience the World

We rarely stop to really look or listen to what is around us and yet subconsciously our brains are dealing with this information and using it to form the basis of thoughts, decisions and actions. Every moment something happens, we are evaluating it; how it feels, what we think about it and whether it poses any threat to our survival. Our mind and body are ready to take whatever primal action is needed to protect us.

Our mind is interpreting everything we see, feel and experience, *right now,* based on what has happened in our past. It's like having a unique library of programmes that our mind accesses to assess what to do next.

To make this visual, imagine that you are standing on top of a hill. Engrained into that hill are all your life experiences and lessons. As you view the world, you are processing that information and unconsciously making decisions based upon your hill's unique set of references. Let me illustrate this more graphically.

Our Hilltop of Experience

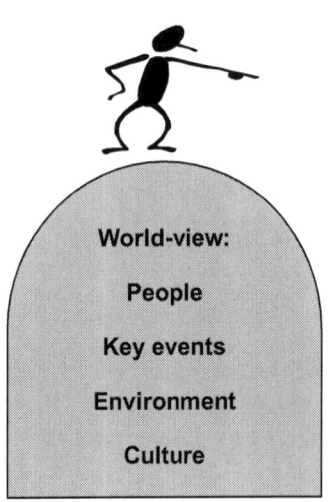

World-view:

People

Key events

Environment

Culture

Four main factors shape our view of the world: people, events, environment and culture. Our experiences of these factors then influence our beliefs, values, attitudes and behaviours, many of which remain with us throughout our lives if left unchallenged.

From the moment we are born, what we experience begins to construct our hilltop and influence the way we handle situations.

As infants our brains are constantly taking in information although it is not sophisticated enough to critically evaluate the 'good' from the 'bad'. We absorb everything and our deep-rooted, subconscious patterns and beliefs about ourselves start to form. This becomes our hard-drive where all our programmes, determining our future actions, are stored.

The belief is that by age seven, we have already formed the unique features of our personality and behaviour patterns. Whilst subsequent life events continue to influence us, our main programmes have been set.

These programmes influence how we deal with every situation we face from our ability to walk, to our self-discipline whilst on a diet or our subtle sabotage of New Year's Resolutions. They also shape how we interact with danger or threat, how we handle conflict and our reaction to bad news.

Four Factors Influencing our Hilltop

People

Our parents or guardians are major influences. They are the first people we see, who are responsible for our upbringing and who start shaping how we see the world. They contribute to creating our 'truths'.

Latest science suggests that their influence can even precede birth. During pregnancy, life's events have an impact on parent's physiology and emotions and the unborn baby picks up on each of their vibrations.

The more familiar science suggests their influence is most significant after birth. We watch, listen, learn and even download their language to our subconscious memory. As a result, our parent's beliefs and philosophies become ours.

People often ask me how two siblings can have completely different beliefs, perceptions and behaviours. This is easy to answer. Child 1 is born to new parents who have no experience or training in parenthood. Child 2 is born to parents who have grown into their role, thereby influencing the second child with a different set of experiences. The result is that the younger child's hilltop will be different to their elder sibling.

A point to acknowledge; we must not blame our parents. When we understand the roots of our programming and realise that we can change how we respond to those programmes, we take responsibility for improving our 'lot' rather than becoming victims of the past or our parents.

We must, of course acknowledge the role family, friends, teachers and other authority figures have on our programming. Everyone we had a significant connection to in our childhood leaves an impression on our hard-drive.

I found as an only child that I came to value solitude and even today, my independent streak can be rooted to having no siblings. I also have a strong memory of my Geography teacher. He had a fierce determination to ensure we all passed **his** exam and this reinforced my programme about not letting people down, fearing failure and therefore creating a pressure to succeed.

Events

This covers a broad range of historical incidents that extend from family deaths, bullying, illness and some of those unspeakable events that haunt us; to less intense events like house moves, changing schools or rows with friends. Each event may just be a moment in time or months in the unfolding, although each forms an impression on our hilltop.

One powerful event I often replay from my childhood is of three inseparable friends at Junior School who, one day had a disagreement. In the heat of the argument, the two girls paired up and left me alone. Whilst we made up, the event left an indelible mark on me and I return to this as a key event in the formation of my *people pleasing* and *avoidance* behaviour. Deep in my conditioning, I have a programme

27

that says people will leave me after a row, so avoid conflict at all costs so that I am not abandoned. How interesting!

I remember one client describing the impact that growing up in a Care Home had on him. He recognised that to survive he had learned to be ruthless, strong and dominant and these behaviours remained with him into his career. Once he realised the root of his behaviour, he was able to take control and learn a more constructive way of interacting - this one realisation changed his whole outlook on life and his work impact.

Environment

This is all about the setting and atmosphere surrounding us as a child. So for example, our family's size and gender make up, our position with our siblings, the family dynamic and culture.

Was it a noisy, energising family environment, with people always moving, talking and playing? Or was it a peaceful environment that brought out a reflective nature? We could extend this to cover the environment in which we lived; whether a village or town? How safe was our street – did we feel safe playing outside until dark? Did we live on an island, in the country, down a remote lane or inner city? All these affect the way we see and experience the world today.

Culture

Culture is the ideas, customs and social behavioural characteristics of a particular group or society who create a set of spoken or unspoken 'truths' about the nature of that group.

That definition provides good logic for why culture determines our subconscious programming. Depending upon our country or city of birth, our family's religious beliefs or clubs we join, each play a unique part in moulding how we think and behave. The group's collective views, 'truths' and rules provide a structure for how we operate together and so, through repetitive exposure, we begin to absorb those rules into our own philosophies and they provide a benchmark for how we live our lives.

Hilltop Exercise

Reflect on what has shaped your hilltop, using the four headings. Identify what key elements have conditioned you to see the world as you do.

This is a powerful exercise, so do take care whilst you work through it, as some difficult connections may arise for you. If this happens, perhaps just write it down and then leave it for a while before trying to understand its impact on you.

If thinking about historical specifics is too difficult, then you could change the way you review your influences by using the present. Take one of your current behavioural traits and ask, 'What has happened in the past that has influenced me to behave in this way today?'

The hilltop is such a powerful tool for understanding why we do what we do and really does help us make some important connections.

Other People's Hilltops

So far, we have used the hilltop analogy as a tool for self-assessment. This also works for understanding other people's hilltops. As we explore assertiveness further, especially in the third section, we revisit this notion and use it as a tool for developing greater appreciation of others and avoiding conflict and confrontation.

"Give me a child of seven and I will show you the man."

Jesuit saying

Chapter 4
Building your Jigsaw

"Knowing others is intelligence, knowing yourself is true wisdom."

Lao Tzu

We are piecing together some important elements of our personal jigsaw, which is helping us to understand ourselves better. Now we need some structure to form a bigger picture – if you like the corner pieces to our assertive jigsaw. This chapter is highly interactive and so I encourage taking time to think about what the questions mean.

When we understand what is at the heart of our behaviour, attitudes and decisions, we find clarity and realisation knocking on our door, offering us options to change.

Personal Building Blocks

We are made up of many different aspects that can best be described as building blocks and to illustrate this I would like to use the analogy of a tree: A tree is organised into a number of key components that enable it to function.

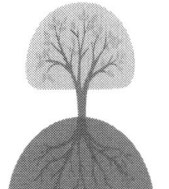

The Roots: provide the tree's nourishment, running deep underground and rarely seen by the onlooker. They are vital to the very essence of the tree's existence, to its vitality and keeping it anchored and safe.

The Trunk and Branches: provide the tree's stability and structure, which are essential for transporting the nutrients from roots to leaves.

The Foliage: defines the tree's identity. How it flourishes depends on many things, although without its interaction with the roots and trunk, the foliage suffers and presents an unhealthy image.

Using this imagery, we can now see how these layers relate to us:

Inner Core: like the tree's root system, we too have a deeply engrained, invisible network of needs, conditioning, values, beliefs and principles that subconsciously feed and shape our lives.

Mind-sets: driven by our inner core, our attitudes, philosophies and perspectives take shape, affecting how we react to the world.

Behaviours: this is the external display of our inner programmes and portrays our identity and image. Through our vocal, verbal and habitual patterns, we project an image and create interactions that form the basis of our relationships.

When we understand the intricate interplay of these three layers, we get a real sense of how they represent us. The following exercises help us explore each of these layers to create a more profound self-understanding and open the door for change.

Your Roots – Inner Core

There are many rooted elements we could explore, although from my coaching perspective there are two essential activities. Firstly, I encourage you to look at your values, the cornerstone of your decisions. Secondly, I ask you to assess your needs and drivers to see how they trigger your primal behaviour patterns.

Values

Values are like having a personal compass. They are deep-rooted standards that form in childhood and evolve as we age. They are the basis on which we structure our attitudes, are the source of our actions and the foundation of our choices.

If our values differ to either family members or friends, it can create conflict. In fact, if at any point in our lives, we feel unhappy, just check out how aligned we are to our values. I suspect that one of them is out of kilter and once we restore that value's priority, our conflict disappears.

I remember a client telling me how miserable she felt at home and when we explored why, we uncovered that she placed a high value on organisation and order. Unfortunately, her husband didn't share this value, which created conflict between them. She realised that her need for order was verging on an unhealthy obsession as it impacted elsewhere in her life. We unearthed that one of her hilltop experiences had created a deep-rooted fear of danger and vulnerability and so to protect herself from harm, she had developed a strong value around control and order.

This insight gave her a different perspective about her values and their impact, enabling her to adjust the significance she placed on them. This helped her have a meaningful conversation with her husband about how she felt and they found a compromise that created the order she craved.

By assessing our values, we are able to see where conflicts come from; gauge the impact that dishonouring our values has and leads to better quality relationships with those around you.

Before I ask you to consider your values, here is an insight into my **core values**:

Choice Simplicity Making a difference Family Love Integrity Gratitude Health

My peripheral values are:

Adventure Independence Exploration Privacy Nature Structure Security Creativity

These, albeit on the periphery, still matter to me, although they have less dominance in my decision-making. As circumstances change, these peripheral values may become more important.

Values Exercise

 Take some time to reflect upon and then highlight as many of the words from the list on the next page that strike a chord with you. Avoid spending too much time thinking about them and go with your instinct. This initial list represents your **peripheral values**.

Now identify your **core values** by selecting your **top seven** from that list. These core values will be the words or statements that mean the most to you or have the greatest significance for you.

If you only selected seven values in the first part of this exercise, then prioritise your top three core values.

Finally, if you had to pick **the one, most important value** for you, which would it be? How does this value influence your decision-making and your behaviours?

Which values do you feel are currently out of balance and which do you feel totally aligned to and comfortable with?

- Peace
- Independence
- Ambition
- Friendship
- Being analytical
- Boundaries
- Making decisions
- Work promotion
- Leadership
- Integrity
- Pressure
- Self-expression
- Isolation
- Nurturing
- Recognition
- Team playing

- Pleasing people
- Adventure
- Innovation
- Expertise
- Flexibility
- Problem-solving
- Collaboration
- Family and friends
- Knowledge
- Attention to detail
- Caring
- Decisiveness
- Physical challenge
- Connection
- Precision
- Excitement and fun

- Variety
- Competition
- Freedom
- Status
- Creativity
- Order & control
- Taking risks
- Security & safety
- Money
- Challenge
- Routine
- Community
- Dominance
- Travel
- Perfectionism
- Helping others

Six Basic Human Needs

Our needs form part of a subconscious network of intrinsic drivers that trigger us to act in a primal way. They are more than, 'I need a new car.' They are yearnings created by our early hilltop experiences and which create a reflexive behaviour aimed at fulfilling those needs.

The following model, adapted from author Tony Robbins helps explain the role our needs have in shaping our behaviours. When I first carried out this exercise, the penny dropped. It explained two things: firstly, why I was so passionate about my job, given the height of my **need for contribution** and secondly, why I needed so much structure and control in my life, given my **need for certainty**.

Six Basic Human Needs

- Certainty
- Uncertainty
- Significance
- Connection/community
- Contribution (adding value)
- Growth

Certainty: is the assurance of something happening or not happening. For example, the need to know that the car will start or having a daily routine that presents no surprises, thereby allowing us to give our best.

Uncertainty: conversely is the excitement of the unknown and the need for variability. As an example, we may go on holiday without booking any accommodation – we 'go where the fancy takes us.' A leader would love the diversity of working with different cultures and would hate the regimented structure that others needing certainty would crave.

Significance: is the need to be remembered, to be important and for our lives to mean something. Examples might a politician or a scientist like Albert Einstein.

Connection: is the need to be part of a community or group and share in the meaning of their connection. This is about acceptance, inclusion and feeling cared for. We see examples of people joining community groups like work's Social or Charity Committee or Parent Teacher Associations and UK's Women's Institute as part of a need to belong.

Contribution: is the altruistic need to make a difference to someone or something. People with a high contribution need are driven by activities that add real value to someone's life.

Growth: is all about the desire to learn, develop and improve. We often find people with a high growth need taking on extra studies or exams in their personal time, even when they seem overloaded.

Six Basic Human Needs Exercise

Using these descriptions, consider the order of your needs. You may find it easier to start with the highest and lowest and then work out your middle needs, as these can be harder to differentiate.

When you are happy with your order, journalise the impact your heirachy has on your behaviours – how do you behave to fulfil your top ranking needs?

Your Trunk – Mind-sets

As we return to the tree analogy, we can begin to explore the role the trunk has on our make up.

The trunk and branches provide the backbone to our behaviour; namely our attitudes, emotions, perspectives and perceptions. Essentially, how we feel and think about the world.

We look more closely at how we think in Part 2, so I don't want to spoil the surprise in this section, although mindsets and emotions are certainly worth our attention.

Mind-sets and Thinking Styles

How we view things is so important to how we behave. Recall a time when everything seemed to be going wrong. How many destructive ideas and assumptions were running through your mind at that time? What impact did they have on you and on the people around you?

When we hold unhealthy assumptions about others or ourselves it can have a disturbing effect on our behaviour. It is like wearing a set of glasses that are out of focus; our view can become distorted and we risk our misconceptions affecting our relationships, our health and our professional reputation.

Imagine we are visiting a new country; we quickly accumulate impressions of what we see and develop views based on our previous experiences. We then form an opinion and perhaps a judgement on the culture, the people and its architecture. We may even find ourselves comparing it to other countries we have been to and using that perspective to draw some unfair conclusions.

Now imagine we are visiting that same country with a friend who has a completely different perspective to us. They develop their own set of notions and assumptions shaped by their previous experiences and therefore see it differently to us. Which perspective is right?

Both are right and both viewpoints are relevant. Our challenge is to appreciate that a different opinion is just as valid and the difference doesn't make either person wrong.

It shows us there is another way - a different view and more than one way of seeing things. It is good to acknowledge our current viewpoint on certain topics and then develop a willingness to accept that there are other ways to see things.

This can help tremendously as we begin to form a more flexible approach that gives equal space to everyone's opinions without having to judge them as right or wrong; they are just different.

Here are some powerful questions we can ask to expand our mind-set:

How else could I think about this?

How would someone else see this?

What is the alternative view?

These alternatives help flex our mental muscle, challenging us to expand our perspective and to search for a viewpoint that helps us feel more constructive during our interactions.

Crooked Styles of Thinking

Our thoughts influence how we feel and this affects how we think. This partnership is quite dramatic in the way it shapes our behaviour. Our thoughts are incredibly powerful, as we will see in the next section and they have the ability to shape how we behave, the quality of feeling we have about others and that we have about ourselves. Ultimately, they influence the type of future we have.

Often we just think of our thoughts as being 'negative' and that is all there is to it. Although in the spirit of self-awareness, it's important to assess the different type of negative thoughts that plague our minds, as each one has a slightly different role that influences a completely different range of emotions and, therefore, behaviours. Here are the styles:

The Catastrophe	Over-generalising
Predicting the worst outcome.	Assuming that because something happened once, it will happen again.
Exaggerating	**Discounting the Positive**
Giving events more importance than is deserved.	Rejecting the good as if it did not count.

Mind Reading	Predicting the Future
Believing that you know what others are thinking.	Fortune telling what you image to happen in the future.
Black and White Thinking	**Taking Things Personally**
Swtiching from one extreme to another.	Always seeing the attack on your character.
Taking the Blame	**Emotional Reasoning**
Taking responsibility that isn't yours.	Mistaking feelings for facts.
Name Calling	**Scare Mongering**
Involving either yourself or others.	An irrational perspective that is just an illusion.
Wishful Thinking	
Things would be better if they only they were different.	

Crooked Styles of Thinking Exercise

Which of the thinking styles listed above can you relate to most? Over the next couple of days, start to take more notice of your thinking styles and the mind-set that you adopt most often. Observe the type of feelings they provoke and then the resulting behaviour.

Also, watch out how those mind-sets influence the relationships around you. This is all incredibly helpful evidence that enables you to instigate change for the better.

Your Foliage – Behaviour

The final part of our tree concept is the foliage, which consists of everything visible to others, on which they form an impression. This includes: our body language, facial expressions, style of dress, our voice and words. This behaviour can be split into two elements; **our reactions**, which are instinctive and **our responses**, which are reasoned and rational. When developing assertion, it is of course the latter on which we must focus.

Reaction Formula

The key to our assertion is moving away from that primal **fight and flight** reaction to a considered response. Here's a Reaction Formula that illustrates the interplay between our innate thoughts, feelings and behaviours.

$$\textit{Trigger - (Thought + Feeling) x Behaviour = Interaction}$$

The best way to bring this to life is to describe a personal situation that thankfully is now resolved, although illustrates how the formula works.

My unhealthiest pattern was road-rage - here's the chain of events:

Trigger   A car would overtake me under dangerous conditions or flash me to move over.

Thought   'What an idiot, don't you know how much danger you're causing?' Alternatively, 'How dare you flash me, I'm not driving slowly.' Or, 'You incompetent, crazy *****. Don't you know how ridiculous that was?'

Feeling   Anger, rage, irritation, resentment.

Behaviour   The combination of my instantaneous thoughts and feelings resulted in an aggressive outpouring of gesticulations, flashing and horn honking, accelerating, driving up close and risking my life and others.

Interaction	My reactions to this event could have triggered, in the protagonist, their own rage, forcing me to stop my car and having a high-risk altercation. Although, generally this resulted in a return of gesticulations, horn blasting and further speeding.
Result	This pattern of anger would stay with me for hours, carrying the emotion home and taking it out on my husband. He left wondering what he had done wrong and I felt awful, because I felt out of control.

So what do we do about this? We learn how to *interrupt the pattern.*

Interrupting the Pattern

1. Firstly, we need to understand what **triggers** us to think and feel a certain way. Understand what really 'makes us mad'; what buttons are pushed to 'make our blood boil.'

2. Next, examine how to change the **thought** into something less destructive. For example, we could **flip the thought** into something more positive, 'No harm done.' We could turn it into a question, which develops a more rational perspective where we limit the intensity of our emotion and prevent the chain reaction; 'I wonder what's going on for them today?'

3. We could interrupt at the **feeling** by acknowledging how we feel. A simple, 'I feel really angry about what's just happened.' By taking ourselves back into a thought, we have interrupted the behaviour cycle and immediately moved into something more rational.

4. The most important interruption is to our **behaviour**. *Realising we have a choice about the way we behave* is vital, because when we take responsibility for our actions, our behaviours change.

"No one can make you feel anything without your consent."
Eleanor Roosevelt

Responding not Reacting

The final part of our foliage is to make the distinction between a **primal reaction** and an **assertive response**. Stephen Covey in his book, *'Seven habits for highly effective people'* states this as the **freedom to choose**.

We all have this basic freedom and yet how often do we exercise it? Realising we have the option to choose our thoughts and responses is empowering and is an essential ingredient to our assertion. Understanding what *influences* us is important, and so too is the realisation that we can take responsibility for our actions and thoughts.

The **freedom to choose** is about developing a **habit of proactivity**. This means taking responsibility for our behaviour and our destinies. So rather than blaming others and things that are out of our control, we need to recognise the importance of responsibility and how we can initiate an alternative result by choosing to respond in a different way.

If we allow our lives to be a result of our conditioning, we subconsciously empower them. When we react, we let such things as the weather influence how we feel, we allow others to treat us disrespectfully and then blame them for how we feel. It is not their fault. We have a choice.

Being proactive means we take responsibility for our actions and recognise that we can choose how we respond based on our values and not a set of external factors. When we realise that we have the ability **to feel a certain way**; **to think a certain way**; **to respond in a certain way** at any moment in time then we reap assertive rewards.

"Wisdom is knowledge applied."

Elyse Killoran, Coach

Chapter 5
The Magnificent Seven

*"There is only one corner of the Universe that you can be
certain of improving and that is your own self."*

Aldous Huxley

I guess if I was in your shoes right now, I would be screaming, 'So tell me how I do it.' I realise that this first part of the book has been a big ask. I have appealed to your reflective nature and asked you to be patient and, in many ways, to trust me to show you how to unlock the real issues holding back your assertion. Our instinct is so often to **do** and thereby **fix**, rather than **think and plan how to fix**.

This chapter rewards your patience with the presentation of seven powerful strategies that have a proven track-record in my Assertiveness Workshops and helped clients master the art of authentic assertion.

This magnificent seven is not, of course the final prescription by any means. Part 3 gives even more situational specific techniques. Although in my experience, I have found that by mastering these simple strategies and building on our self-awareness, we have plenty in our toolkit to make a difference.

My hope is that after reading this first enlightening section that we can take some time to absorb, reflect and deepen our awareness. By investing time in applying some of these seven strategies and observing their effect, we begin to get a sense of what is working and what still needs refining. Once we have mastered the techniques, we will then be ready to take the next few steps on the path to authentic assertion.

Thinking Strategies

I have grouped the following three strategies into approaches for our **mind**. By thinking differently, we behave differently. Here is a mental muscle workout.

Circles of Influence

Adapted from Stephen Covey's model, this first strategy is about prioritising where we invest our energy and limiting the amount we worry.

When we realise what is in our control to change or influence we begin to see challenges and problems through completely different lenses. We start to develop proactive thinking and let go of a whole heap of 'stuff' that get us down.

Let's face it, we all have different things that cause us worry and anxiety. I think about my and my family's health; whether my readers will gain value from my books; the amount of Genetically Modified Organism's (GMOs) in our food.

Using the following strategy, Circles of Influence and other models, I have learnt to manage my mind, to a large degree, and so my worries are less intense.

Other worries might include money, family safety, meeting deadlines, traveling, difficult work issues or the latest tax allowances. Some of these we can tackle, whilst others are less in our power to change.

Circles of Influence helps categorise what we worry about into three areas:

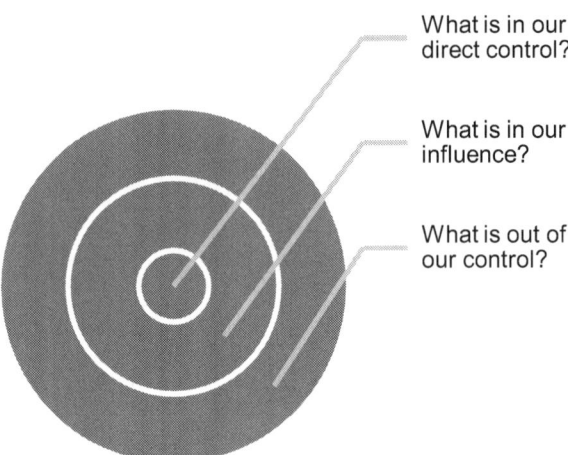

What is in our direct control?

What is in our influence?

What is out of our control?

What is in our Direct Control?

This includes all the things that we have both the right and opportunity to change immediately, anything that concerns us and our surrounding environment that doesn't involve anyone else directly. This encompasses how we respond, how we think and how we feel.

My health worries triggered me to attend Health seminars and I studied Naturopathic Nutrition and read health-oriented books. This helped me see my well-being in a different light and consequently my worry has decreased because I changed what was in my direct control.

What is in our Influence?

There will undoubtedly be things we worry about that we have little or no responsibility to change, typically involving other people. We waste so much energy trying to persuade them to see our view and then get frustrated when they ignore us. Yet we only have the right to change ourselves.

There will also be situations outside our control that we allow to cause us anxiety. We cannot directly control this and if we tried, it would most likely create a confrontation. For example, an issue between two friends that causes an atmosphere amongst the group – we worry about the effect it has on everyone and we want to fix it.

So instead, realise that although we cannot change it or them, we can influence the situation, through conversations, feedback and being open and honest. Perhaps we could talk to our friends about what's going on individually and help them work through the problems. Then step back and let them resolve the challenges between them.

When I realised there was little I could do to control my family's health, my worry changed. After all, their health is their responsibility. What I can do though is share my knowledge and through my influence and good practice hope that they take the opportunity to improve their lifestyle. When I let go of this need to make it right for others, my anxiety lessened in intensity.

What is out of our Control?

The third category incorporates those things that are completely out of our control, yet invest a disproportionate amount of time worrying about. This might include global warming, our PC crashing, nuclear war threats, the Government's decision on Tax rises or the threat of redundancy.

My worries over GMOs; although an increasing concern, I cannot change Government policy over this directly. Could I influence it in any way? Perhaps I could work with groups who are trying to stop GM crops. In a more direct way, I could research modified foods that may be in my diet and remove them or better still, just grow my own!

Rather than worrying, take direct control of what we can do, rather than over-dramatising the issue and wasting energy. Invest our energies more wisely and focus on what we can control or influence and if there is nothing we can do, then let it go.

How Many Squares?

For those of us on Facebook, we may have seen this doing the rounds. The exercise simply asks us to count the squares. What number do we come up with? 16, 17, 21,or 25? My answer is **30** when to take into account the **one** whole square, the **sixteen** small squares, the **nine** 2x2 squares and the **four** 3x3 squares.

Irrespective of our answer there is an interesting moral to the story. It is not so much how many squares we see, rather how many more than sixteen can we see?

Do we:

- only see what is immediately in front of us or can we..
- see beyond and appreciate the bigger picture?

It is too easy to make instant judgements that blind us from what is really there. Those perceptions can dangerously limit our potential and all because we don't look beyond what is in front of us.

So avoid 'Judging a book by its cover.' Be prepared to have an open mind to people, things and events and be more inquisitive, before we pass judgement. We will have a better quality experience.

Hilltops Revisited

For this strategy, I would like to return to Chapter 3, where I introduced the concept of a hilltop, made up of our life's experiences that collectively shape how we see the world.

That principle asked us to focus on *our* hilltop. Now, as a specific thinking strategy, I would like to explore *other people's* hilltops and learn the art of appreciation.

One of the key ingredients to assertion is developing a greater appreciation of people's differences. When we realise it is ok to be different and we embrace that difference, it frees us up from our judgements and criticisms to behave in a more assertive way.

The expanded hilltop concept allows us to do this. Return to our personal hilltop reflections and consider whether our boss, our closest friend or our partner has the same hilltop as us. Whilst they will have the same four headings, their experiences will be completely different.

Suddenly their hilltop has a very different formation to ours. Their views, assumptions, mind-sets and behaviours will match their unique experiences, and hence their interpretation of the world will be completely unlike ours.

As an assertive strategy, it's worth taking time to review how the hilltop concept explains the reason for a conflict and what may drive someone's interaction, based on their experiences.

Not all our relationships will be robust enough to allow us to get to know the intimate details of someone's hilltop, although simply knowing that theirs is likely to be different can be enough. Learning to appreciate other's uniqueness is an art, and definitely a strategy to apply when trying to form better quality relationships and when working through confrontation.

Behaving Strategies

This series of four strategies focuses on **doing** something different to improve our success.

Monkey Let Go!

This is my personal favourite and a strategy I use often. Ten years ago, I attended a Meditation course run by a Buddhist monk. Inspirational stories filled his training, which I still share to this day and the monkey is one that stands out.

I am pleased to say that the following story is fictional. It tells of how the ancient Japanese captured monkeys as part of the fur trade. It is said that hunters went into the forest to lay traps in the ground. They carefully dug a hole, deep and wide enough to place a narrow-necked jar into it. They placed the jar in the hole and then covered around it with soil, leaving the jar's neck still visible.

The hunters cut up an apple, placed it into the jar and took their leave, returning to the village for a glass of Saki. Meanwhile, the monkeys ventured down to the forest floor so they could capture their prize. Surely, it was too easy.

The monkeys gingerly placed their hands into the jar and reached for the apple. Gathering up as many of the pieces as they could, they started to pull out their hands, motivated by the awaiting feast. Alas, their hands were so full of apple that they could no longer fit through the jar's neck.

Try as they might, they could not pull out from the jar and return to the safety of their trees, armed with their treasure. Yet with grit and determination they held onto that apple, hoping that some divine intervention would release them from their trap. Little did they realise that just simply letting go of the apple would secure them their freedom, which was about to be stolen.

After a while, the hunters returned to the forest to find the monkeys still working out an escape route and in one simple move, the monkeys were slain and the next trap set.

If only the monkeys had released the apple, they would have been free to live their lives. Sadly, they paid the price of holding onto something they thought was important, yet kept them trapped and finally paying the ultimate price.

So I put it to you... how many apples are you holding onto that cause you headaches? What would happen if you let go of those unnecessary issues or worries? What freedom could you experience by just letting go?

After hearing this story, I found myself unclenching my fist at the slightest worry, symbolically letting go of what held me captive. To this day, my husband sees me worrying and says, 'Karen, just let go of the monkey!' Now he doesn't have quite the right imagery, although the point still stands.

As Richard Carlson writes in his book,

'Don't sweat the small stuff.'

Traffic Lights – Three Little Words

It is the simplicity of this strategy that me and my clients love, combining a bit of thinking and doing.

Whilst I appreciate that whatever country we live in, our traffic lights may have a slightly different sequence - it is the colours I'm more interested in than the light pattern per se. The essence of the Traffic Light theory is that it helps us change from a reaction to a response mechanism.

Picture the scene. We're sat amongst our family when a debate arises between two members. They look to us for our input, what do we do? Our natural instinct is to join the foray, adding our views **or** to freeze, feeling 'put on the spot'. Either way, both reactions are unhealthy and unconstructive.

Here is an alternative:

At red, Stop. Bite our tongue, breathe, mentally hold ourselves back from interjecting or say, 'I need to think about this., to buy ourselves some time.

At amber, Think. Consider the options, given the characters involved and the outcome we want. Think about the consequence of those options and what feels most comfortable for us. This is generally processed in moments, although it might feel like forever.

At green, Choose. Having invested in good quality thinking time, we are ready to choose the best approach, with an increased assurity of a better outcome. Although this is of course, never guaranteed, we will at least improve our chances of success.

Three little words: **Stop, Think, Choose**. These prevent us from speaking out inappropriately or saying nothing when we really want to contribute.

The Power of Questions

Marketers and advertisers use them. Coaches and trainers use them. Journalists use them. **Questions**! I believe **questions**, **listening** and **playback** are three of the most important life-skills we can learn. Once we have mastered these, we open up a whole new dimension of better quality relationships and successful results.

When we master the art of asking good quality questions, rather than making statements, and I mean old-fashioned **open questions,** we begin to unlock the key to our assertive success. Do you remember Rudyard Kipling's poem?

"I kept six honest serving men; they taught me all I knew. Their names were what and why and where and when and where and who."

Learn to use questions more wisely and explore with people. Engage in meaningful conversations through the art of questioning and listening and watch relationships blossom.

Mars Bar Brinciple - Balance

I am sure you have heard the Mars advert so many times in years gone by:

'A Mars and day helps you work, rest and play.'

This is a marketing strap-line, which has been around for decades promoting the Mars Bar, although what has this to do with assertive development?

Quite a lot really, because the advert suggests that the chocolate gives us the energy and sustenance to fulfil all areas of our lives and not be a slave to one or another. In other words giving us what we need to achieve a better life balance. (From a nutritional view point I challenge this, although that aside, my focus is the principle of the advert!)

We can therefore use the analogy to help us connect with assertiveness's lure of greater energy, positivity, calmness, esteem and balance. All of which free us up to live and work to our full potential rather than living on our all-too-often frayed edge of existence.

Now, I am not suggesting for a minute that we eat a Mars Bar a day, although when we invest in the Mars principle and rebalance the way that we think, feel and behave, we will have all the fuel we need to feel fulfilled.

This brings us to the end of Chapter 5 and what I hope has been an interesting meander through the nursery beds of our assertive landscape. More of this will come in Part 3, where we expand our exploration into specific situations that require a more assertive approach.

In the meantime, I genuinely hope that this *inside-out* philosophy has opened up a completely new aspect of assertiveness and how, what we have experienced in the past shapes how we behave today. With our new insights, I now invite the completion of this first phase of our fascinating introspective journey, with some action planning.

"Knowing alone is not good enough. You need to apply what you know if you want to change."

Karen Davies, Coach

Chapter 6
Setting Goals for Change

"Before you score you must first have a goal."

Proverb

Much has been reported on studies that show the relationship between goal setting and success. In my coaching experience when there is enough desire to change, then this creates a momentum that needs no pressure, forcing or pushing.

Desire creates an innate propulsion that carries us forward. Armed with a clear focus on what we want to be different, commitment to see it through and hard work, we can turn our dreams into reality.

The most successful clients and participants have been those so determined to change that they don't need to make pledges to anyone else except themselves. They've reached a point where there are no doubts about whether to take action – it's been about **what** action am I going to take?

And so before we waltz gracefully towards Part 2, I would like to suggest some reflection time, as this book is a journey and every journey needs its pit stops.

This section is short and sweet and gives us an opportunity to think about how we translate our learning into something tangible that can make a difference. After all the time we have invested in studying the words and doing the exercises, surely we need to now convert that into something valuable, meaningful and productive?

Six Steps to Making Change Stick

Step 1 – Review your Learning

Reflecting back on the exercises you've completed, think about what stood out for you. There has been plenty to consider, so collecting your thoughts and gathering up what have been the most useful discoveries is an important step before you begin translating those into goals.

Learning Review Exercise

Return to each chapter, noting down the elements that have struck a chord with you.

Then go back to Chapter 2 specifically, where I asked you to consider your vision and what you wanted to achieve by reading this book. Based on that information, what have you learned and discovered?

Step 2 – Review your Goals

As you review your original goals, you may feel that they no longer work or that they are too woolly, especially given your discoveries. Rest assured this is quite natural. Visions and goals need to be flexible and adaptive, so use them as a reference point. If your goals need to change, carry out the Goal Review exercise below, otherwise move on to Step 3.

Goal Review Exercise

If your original goals need to change, rewrite what you want to achieve based on your learning.

Consider what you want to look, sound and feel like in a year's time. With your goals revised, you can return to your learning review notes and identify what will most help you achieve your goals.

Step 3 – Your Inspirations

When we are inspired to do something then nothing stops us. Think back to a time when you've had a real passion, an energy to do say a marathon, bring up a family or work for a charity that's close to your heart. Even though you're busy, you make time for inspirational activities. If you have a high **Need for Growth**, (which we discussed in Chapter 4), then you won't need passion, as you will be inspired enough by your desire to satisfy that need.

Inspired Action

Albert Einstein said, *"Genius is 1% inspiration and 99% perspiration"*. This may be true, yet without inspiration, our perspiration is wasted sweat.

List what you are most inspired to do that will help you towards your newly revised goals in Chapter 2. Only list three things so that you keep focused.

Step 4 – Return Of The 'Six Honest Serving Men'!

In the last chapter I suggested improving the quality of your questioning technique. It is now time to use that skill in setting your action plan.

Taking the three most relevant inspirations, turn each one into a measurable and tangible action using the following six questions.

What: will you specifically do differently?

Why: is this important to you?

How: will you approach achieving this goal?

When: will you do this and over what period?

Who: will need to support you and who do you need to involve?

Where: will this goal take place, home, work, socially?

Step 5 – Do and Review

"We are what we repeatedly do. Excellence then, is not an act, but a habit."

Aristotle

It is now time to take action and **repeated action** at that. Inspired by your commitments, you need to go forth and practise. To help you, here is some guidance about making change long-lasting and not just a 'five minute wonder'.

- **Focus only on three commitments.** If you adopt any more it will become like a shopping list, often overwhelming and soon forgotten. When you have changed those commitments into new habits, then you can identify your next set of actions.

- **Repeat your actions regularly.** The more you repeat an action, the more you hone your skills.

- **Involve people in your changes.** Talk to people close to you about your desired change, especially family and friends. With their inclusion, you secure their support rather than creating fear and suspicion.

- **Carry out regular reviews and write down your successes**. The more you assess your progress and celebrate what is going well, the more momentum you will experience. You will also be more in tune with what is working less well and be able to make adjustments.

- **Celebrate your successes**. It is important to acknowledge what is going well. Share those successes with colleagues, friends who will be interested, your partner or boss. The act of sharing itself reinforces the positivity of the action and inspires you to continue.

Step 6 – Commit to Paper

It's been proved that when we write down our goals, we are more likely to stick to them. So I encourage you to commit your intentions to paper and make them public where you will see them regularly.

Now armed with a dash of knowledge, a splash of hope and a pinch of inspiration, you have all you need to create an authentic assertive change.

I encourage you to use the next **four to six weeks** to experiment, talk, journalise and reflect on what is going well and what still needs some work before you head towards the next exciting instalment in this book.

If this first section has piqued your curiosity, then the second will intrigue you even further. We delve into a critical source of our success; **how we communicate**, both the internal dialogue we call our thoughts, self-talk, fears and doubts; and externally through our interactions with others.

We explore the science of the brain and consider what role it plays in our effectiveness. We discuss how, what you think affects your destiny and how to reframe your mental self-worth programmes to achieve greater results. Armed with a new vocabulary, I show you a process that eradicates your fears, irrational beliefs and self-imposed doubts increasing the quality of what you say to **yourself** and **others** by 100%. You then have a brain cleared for action – positive, purposeful and powerful action.

"The best thing about the future is that it comes one day at a time."

Abraham Lincoln

Part 2

Creating Unshakeable Self-esteem

A Guide to Having Meaningful Conversations

Chapter 1
Introduction

"We are what we think. All that we are arises with our thoughts. With our thoughts we make our world."

Buddha

My philosophy on developing self-confidence and assertiveness is to take an *inside-out* approach, inspired by Stephen Covey's book, *The 7 Habits of Highly Effective People*. When we explore, at a profound level, why we do what we do or think what we think, we are so much closer to becoming the person we are destined to be.

Assertiveness is such a big topic that it needs breaking down into manageable chunks that enables us to create a long-lasting change – hence the approach I have taken.

The first section of this three-part series, I laid down some critical principles for raising our self-awareness, through which we gain a tremendous understanding of our current behaviours and what could be holding us back from that illusive assertive Utopia.

This second section looks at mastering our interactions by exploring how our **dialogue** influences our self-esteem and how others experience us. We discover the role our thoughts have on our self-worth and behaviour patterns and explore some of the latest research that reveals the mind/body association that has exciting potential for the way we utilise our brainpower. In addition, we uncover how to interact more influentially, addressing more than the traditional communication topics we are familiar with, enabling us to earn greater respect and achieve better results.

Setting the Context - The Two Faces of Dialogue

Before we go on, let me be clear what I mean by the word **dialogue** and set the context for this second section. Dialogue has two faces to it:

Firstly, internal dialogue. This consists of the language, beliefs and thoughts that come from our mind and can best be described as *self-talk*. If this is the first time you have come across this term, it may seem an odd label and for many, creates a suggestion of madness. Our internal dialogue has a subtle, yet powerful influence over how we see ourselves. The apparent simplicity of the phrase, "I'm no good at that," has a huge significance over how we perform, how we feel about ourselves and the general quality of our interactions.

Our habitual, internal dialogue forms programmes that, based on the quality of the language we use, unconsciously shapes our self-perceptions. More directly, those 'thought programmes' impact on the way we then behave and interact. Interestingly, science is increasingly affirming the links between mind and body, encouraging us to consider the result our thoughts have on our effectiveness, our health and well-being.

The second face is our interactive dialogue. This is the combination of our words, tone, body language and our intent when we engage with others. We typically refer to this as *communication*, although I feel this is too unsophisticated a term and needs a fresh perspective. The quality of our interactive dialogue affects the condition of our relationships and shapes the response we receive from others.

To increase our effectiveness and well-being, I believe we need to explore *communication* from a new angle; acknowledging the impact that a more inclusive interaction has on our success, our relationships and the overall quality of our lives.

As you can see, **dialogue** differs in its characteristics and role, yet each one has a powerful part to play in our assertion, which we explore in this section.

The Interaction/Assertiveness Partnership

We predominantly see assertiveness as a *behaviour style* that through the implementation of key techniques can achieve win-win outcomes, allowing all parties to feel fairly treated and honoured. Whilst accurate, this notion represents a superficial assertive ideal; be prepared to look deeper within and we find far more answers to our assertive challenges than this classical model offers.

When we are prepared to seek out this deeper connection, we realise that assertiveness is as much about how we treat ourselves as it is about the way we treat others. If we treat ourselves unfairly, then it will be hard to sustain an assertive style with others. In line with my *inside-out* philosophy, assertion must first come from within – once we acknowledge this, then what we project on the outside will be authentic.

The quality of our internal dialogue is a great guide to understanding how we truly regard ourselves. If we portray our worthiness using poor quality internal language, then our behaviours will follow suit. Everything we show to others is a direct reflection of what we think and feel on the inside.

Internal language such as, 'I can't do this', or 'I'm bound to fail', over time can form a self-belief foundation upon which our behaviours sit. If we hold beliefs like these, we display withdrawn body language, our conversations match our self-deprecating language and our tone of voice sounds hesitant, meek and fearful. These features then combine to form an unassertive representation, which is likely to receive an unassertive response from those around us.

We can therefore, begin to see the impact our internal dialogue has on our external interactions. Get the *inside* strong, worthy and the *outside* acts like a mirror, which people respond to positively – this is the strength of their partnership.

Before we start, I would like you to take a few moments to think about why you want to read this section and set some goals for what you would like to learn and experience, which may build on what you have learned from the first section.

Personal Hopes and Expectations

What would you most like to know, understand or appreciate more because of reading this section?

What do you imagine yourself being able to do differently, after your reading?

Given the two faces of Dialogue that I have mentioned, what interaction challenges do you experience most often that you would like to resolve?

"You are what you are and where you are because of what has gone into your mind. You can change what you are and where you are by changing what goes into your mind."

Zig Ziglar

Chapter 2
Internal Dialogue

"Every thought we think is creating our future."

Louise L. Hay

If we build our assertive strength from the inside, then our ability to lead, influence, interact and build meaningful relationships increases. If we fix our assertive challenges with just a few random strategies, then we end up applying a sticking plaster to the issue, which soon returns to haunt us.

I believe that personal development is an inside job and in this second chapter, we focus on the fundamental role our internal dialogue plays in the condition of our self-esteem and the relationship we have with ourselves. When we master our thoughts then we master our happiness, rather than relying on or blaming external factors.

Evolving Science of the Brain and the Mind

There is an increasing interest in how to enhance well- being through making the most of our minds. Four decades ago, Neuro-linguistic-Programming (NLP) introduced us to a physiological phenomenon that helped us master our self-awareness and our relationships with others. Science continues to intrigue us with new developments in the mind-body connection.

This chapter aims to consolidate some of the material that is out there about the brain and our mind, relating this closely to the role they play in our development. Although, let me lay out my boundaries very clearly before we continue, as there is a huge amount of scientific data and detail available to us around this topic. I intend to present just a flavour of the theories, concepts and philosophies, focusing on what I have found most interesting and relevant in my career.

The Small Matter of the Brain

Scientifically, we are much clearer about how the brain and our central nervous system physiologically and chemically run our bodies and their influence on our behaviours. Neuroscience has even revealed evidence that there is a partnership between our emotions and our limbic brain, showing how we subjectively experience and objectively express emotions such as anger, fear, pleasure and joy. Yet, we have only scratched the surface of our brain's capabilities. Even Albert Einstein recognised:

"We do not know one thousandth of one per cent of what nature has revealed to us."

There is a real temptation for me to talk about the brain's biology and chemistry; the interdependent two hemispheres, the four lobes, the central nervous system, neurons, plasticity and brainwaves, all of which could have a deserved place in this chapter.

Although for the purposes of this book, I will focus more on the abstract nature of the mind and the modern physics paradigm that present different ways of understanding the mind-body connection.

Quantum Theory and a Basis for the Mind

The theories of two great Physicists offer an interesting dimension into our Internal Dialogue that are worth touching on, albeit in very crude form; Isaac Newton's theory of the Universe being a machine and Albert Einstein's Quantum Theory based on energy and the electromagnetic spectrum.

Einstein and his colleagues shone an amazing spotlight on a new physics model that has opened up the path for all sorts of advancements in the last century. The basic premise of Quantum Theory, which launched onto the scene in the early 20th Century, has an expansive, interdependent and holistic view of the world and opens up the potential for mind-blowing mind/body connections.

Quantum Theory suggests that everything is energy. All matter is energy and has a frequency, a vibration that can alter the physical and chemical nature of a particle. It is this principle of energy that lays out the premise for how our mind interacts with our body. When the mind has a thought, (which is energy vibrating at a certain frequency), this influences the brain's neurotransmitters and the body's biological functions, which release certain hormones that shape how we express ourselves.

Yet Einstein's theory of electromagnetic energy presents a real intellectual challenge to our Newtonian mechanistic conditioning. It stretches our 'black and white' belief, because energy is both invisible and intangible, which has given rise to great cynicism. Paradoxically, we experience the result of Einstein's discoveries at a very practical level every day, in the form of microwave ovens, CAT scans, mobile phones and television.

Dr David Hamilton in his book, *How your Mind can Heal the Body* says,

"Thoughts, emotions and beliefs are not just subjective ideas in the mind, but cause real chemical and physical changes in the brain and throughout the body."

Although what does this have to do with mastering our self-esteem and assertiveness?

We are about to move into the fascinating realm of mind psychology, an abstract concept that can be difficult to grasp. The problem is that the immaterial nature of the mind does not fit our mechanistic view of the world. Yet in presenting an alternative view of our invisible intellect and its innate power, it allows us to consider the possibilities of mastering our mind/body interaction and consequently the external expression of our thoughts and emotions.

As Bruce Lipton says in his book, *The Biology of Belief*,

> **"Thoughts, the mind's energy, directly influence how the physical brain controls the body's physiology."**

In his book, *The Concept of the Mind*, Gilbert Ryle defined the mind as a *'Ghost in the Machine.'* As we explore this ghost, the invisible energy that we call the mind, we enter into a new field of psychological science that reveals a chocolate box of possibilities.

Science of the Mind

This branch of psychology involves the study of the mind and its processes, incorporating research on intelligence, thought, memory, emotion and behaviour. It enables us to make sense of thinking activities such as perception, problem solving, decision-making and planning. It is within this science faction that the illumination around our internal dialogue opens up an interesting set of personal effectiveness possibilities.

The mind is a common and broad term used to capture a diverse range of thinking activity. The Oxford Dictionary defines the mind as:

> **"The element of a person that enables them to be aware of the world and their experiences, to think and to feel; the faculty of consciousness and thought."**

Understanding the Dual Nature of the Mind

Bringing this back to a practical, day to day level, how familiar is this phrase?

> **"I'm in two minds about it."**

We say this so often and yet rarely consider its meaning. It appears to suggest that in a conflict or a moment of indecision we have one mind telling us to take one action and another saying we must do something else. Which mind do we follow? Which one is right? This can sometimes be interpreted as the *heart mind* or gut instinct, versus the *logical head mind.*

In reality, we have only one mind, yet it has two distinct characteristics as Joseph Murphy states in, *The Power of the Subconscious Mind*, where he describes that we have two spheres of activity within that one mind.

Their distinct characteristics are commonly described as:

- The objective and subjective mind, or
- The conscious and subconscious mind, or
- The surface-self and the deep-self
- The head and heart mind.

For the purposes of this book, I will use *Conscious* and *Subconscious*.

For the sake of clarity and simplicity, I would like to explore what this dual nature of our mind looks like and expand upon a gardening analogy that Joseph Murphy uses.

Conscious Mind – The Seed/plant

Our thoughts, ideas, attitudes and beliefs are like seedlings that we plant. The conscious mind is the thinker, planner, problem-solver, decision-maker and rationaliser. It has an active level of awareness attached to it and it sits in the pre-frontal cortex. Features of our conscious mind include:

- Our creativity
- Judgement and reviewing skills
- Reasoning and validation
- Problem solving
- Awareness
- Where choices happen
- Free will
- Manual control
- Holds our aspirations and dreams.

Subconscious Mind – The Soil

Our subconscious soil supports and nurtures the seedling, irrespective of its type, giving life to it and creating its form. Whatever we sow, the soil receives and responds, and so our garden takes on the form of the seeds that we consistently plant.

Features of our malleable subconscious mind include:

- Runs on automatic pilot
- Looks a bit like a jukebox that stores programmes from past events and people
- Houses learned experiences and taught perceptions, creating habits and patterns
- Is like a hard-drive that has programmes down-loaded onto it from observations and experiences we have been exposed to, predominantly during our first seven years
- Uses external stimuli to create behavioural and emotional reactions
- Instinctive, reflexive reactions are stimulated here
- Is significantly more powerful than our conscious mind
- Our conditioning and limiting beliefs are programmed here
- Creates a subtle yet powerful blueprint by which we live our lives
- Houses our fears and doesn't always reveal our truth
- Automatically runs our body's key processes.

Our Behaviour Patterns – The Garden's Landscape

The subconscious mind runs the show 95% of the time. In addition, this hard-working mind also controls the subtle functioning of the body's processes. Our heart, breath, digestion, senses, blood flow all operate reflexively through the subconscious mind.

What we consistently feed and plant in it, becomes our garden's eventual landscape – our predominant behaviour patterns. Feed it with toxic and unhealthy thoughts and we create a garden full of weeds that spread in wild contagion. Feed it with nourishing, self-affirming thoughts and our garden will have an array of colour and variety.

If we think consistently, 'I can't do it', 'I'm too scared', 'I'm useless, I always get things wrong', these become entrenched in our soil and set the foundation for our behaviours – the external expression we exhibit to others. Our external behaviours are a reflection of our subconscious garden and so cultivating the right landscape is a key to being effective.

Ghandi once said:

"Your thoughts become your words. Your words become your actions. Your actions become your habits. Your habits become your value. Your values become your destiny."

I would add to the front of his quote that:

Your thoughts become your beliefs,

Your beliefs become your words...

Ghandi describes perfectly the relationship between our conscious and subconscious mind. Sow self-deprecating thoughts often enough and they become our truth, which influence how we see the world and how we ultimately interact within it.

The more worrying element is not only do our own thoughts impregnate our subconscious mind, what we see and learn from others filters through to embed its roots. So powerful is our brain that we take on other people's realities and make them our own. This is truly worrying because what if that person's truths are not accurate. Our subconscious mind does not monitor or evaluate what we download, it just soaks up what we choose to believe, whether it is true or not and becomes our self-fulfilling prophecy. When we examine them, so many beliefs we hold about ourselves are false, we have just learned to believe in them.

At school, teachers told me that I was unlikely to pass my Geography exam and they suggested I gave it up for the benefit of my other subjects. This was a tough call for me as I loved Geography and so my teachers agreed to me dropping History, which I enjoyed less.

They said that if I worked hard then I might scrape a pass, although not to hold out much hope. I took two truths from this experience; firstly, I came to believe that I was not academic or capable and that I struggled with my studies; the second was that I needed to work hard to achieve anything.

The hard work ethic I am comfortable with, as it is a value that my parents instilled in me and I believe that being conscientious is honourable, although perhaps I have paid the price for this belief. I suspect that I have missed the notion of effortless effort, until recently.

The 'not academic' perception has remained throughout my life. I have avoided professional studies and procrastinated around what I consider to be, 'clever stuff'. I even hear myself saying, "Well I'm not very academic", almost as if apologising for my lack of capability. Yet if I examine the facts, I do have qualifications (thanks to my conscientiousness); I have secured a profitable career and had fifteen years running my highly successful consultancy. Therefore, my non-academic belief has no foundation, and so I wonder how many opportunities passed me by holding that belief?

How easy it is for our subconscious mind to take on other's perceptions and formulate them as our own? Our mind is certainly a complex system of processes that, when combined form an essential part of what makes us uniquely human.

The most important point to summarise here is that although we have created our mind to be this way, we can re-cultivate it to produce better and healthier results.

Self-esteem versus Confidence

Worthy of comment before we move on is to be clear on the distinction between self-esteem and confidence. It is easy to use one, when we really mean the other and so clarity I believe is vital.

To me, *Self-esteem* is on the inside and *Confidence* is the behaviour we display on the outside. More specifically, *self-esteem* is a phrase used to describe the worthiness with which we accord ourselves. It is the attitudes, beliefs and judgements that we hold about ourselves, which are deeply rooted in our subconscious.

Confidence on the other hand is an external expression, that sometimes mirrors what we feel on the inside, although can be a mask we wear.

You may have come across the notion that if we develop a great confidence, then we have it made. Life will be a breeze if we *'act as if'* we are confident. Yet there is a real danger with this idea; it is just a superficial, external confidence that when attacked by a side-swipe, challenges the very core of our self-worth, and has us crumbling to pieces within seconds.

To embed this idea, let's use an analogy of an iced cake.

The outside presents a beautiful, highly decorated cake. It shows confidence, presence and is incredibly appealing. Yet, if on the inside, behind the icing's façade, there is a soggy sponge cake that in a week is likely to sink, sag or go mouldy, what affect will this have on the cake's image? It starts to crack, fall apart and suddenly lose its appeal.

To me, the essence is about building a robust self-esteem – if you like, a rich fruit cake. If on the inside, we can ensure that our beliefs, thoughts and attitudes toward ourselves are rock solid, we have a great opportunity to influence our conditioning. We can then create strong self-worth and project an authentically confident outside that remains intact, robust and resilient, even in the face of adversity.

Impact of Inner Belief and Dialogue

Imagine we had a friend's child to stay with us. What impact would it have on them if we criticised them, put them down and consistently told them off? What would we notice about their body language, behaviours and confidence? We would be likely to see them gradually withdrawing, shying away from you and looking fearful when we spoke.

What do we think is the result of using the same approach towards ourselves? We would get exactly the same result; withdrawal, uncertainty, depressed body language and interactions.

Yet, this is what many of us do to ourselves all too often – generally without realising it. Perhaps during our childhood we heard parents, teachers or authority figures saying, 'You're no good', 'You're stupid', 'That is a ridiculous thing to say'. Those statements, when heard repeatedly, become stories that we play out from our subconscious mind, which then turn into beliefs. Through a conditioned learning process, neural pathways hardwire to respond in a specific way and through repetition become our behavioural patterns.

Like playing a CD, we hear a song repeatedly and come to know the tune, the message and the words off by heart. We merrily hum the tune all day and it lodges in our mind and becomes grooved in our head. The impact of our inner belief system and our internal dialogue on our self-esteem is the same. We are constantly creating our personal internal playlist, which is great, if the tunes are all upbeat and bouncy. If they are morose, downcast and negative, then they have a detrimental impact on our interactions, other's reactions and ultimately our self-esteem.

If we think about it, a baby is born with immense potential, so what happens to create low self-esteem? Our early experiences teach us how to value ourselves; people around us influence our conditioning and help shape our stories.

From those stories we construct judgements about how the world works, filtering out anything that contradicts those stories. We form generalisations, scripts and programmes that embed themselves in our subconscious mind and impact upon every decision we make and every action we take.

Beliefs though, are just beliefs – they do not have objective reality – they form subjectively in our minds, shaping the stories that we live out. The challenge is that having created our inner programmes, which form the foundation of our reality, we then generate or attract situations where we can live out those beliefs, such that they reinforce our truth.

All this shapes our inner critic. Intrinsically this can either positively foster or limit our world-view and therefore shape our success, happiness and achievements. If we do not respect ourselves, how can we fully respect others and how can they truly respect us? If we criticise ourselves, we are more likely to criticise others and in turn, we attract criticism from others.

Noticing the seeds we are planting is critical to our self-esteem, our behaviours and the future we create. If we plant seeds that turn into weeds, this affects the soil and the garden's landscape.

As Michael Kewley writes it in his book, *Life Changing Magic*

"As human beings we are nothing more than the accumulation of the conditioning we have received, the overwhelming majority of which is negative."

Observing the Mind - Exercise

Each day, we have over 50,000 thoughts. Some of which are practical about how to carry out the day's tasks, others are regrets about yesterday, some are hopes for tomorrow. The rest have some impact on our subconscious mind and the soil we are preparing. Getting to know what type of negative thoughts we allow to dirty our mind is important to the elimination exercise we will do later.

I therefore encourage us to be an observer of our mind and catch those self-deprecating thoughts, the self-beliefs and stories that we are running. They are easiest to notice, when we are in a difficult situation. Start to take notice of the ***before*** and ***after*** moments and write down the thoughts that emerge. We will make use of these later in the book.

Self-esteem and Assertion

By now, we will be getting some idea about how having a low opinion of ourselves can affect our behaviour, happiness and the quality of our relationships. As we read in the previous section, doing an *inside job* is a key to our success and happiness; otherwise, we put a sticking plaster on the matter and never really move forward.

We continue the *inside-out* approach with this deep-rooted issue and my belief is that if we can build our self-esteem, from the inside, then our assertive challenges diminish.

I worked with a client who had difficulties with his elder brother, who he was in business with. He was condescending, over-powering and impatient. His demands made my client feel uncomfortable, compromised and small. Whenever his brother asked him to do something, he felt a fear of failure and pressure to get the job done. This was particularly tough for him as a perfectionist, and consequently he put so much energy into pleasing him that he often let others down, who also needed his input.

My client soon realised that his inefficiency was rooted in how he felt around his brother. When he observed his thoughts, he learned that after a request, he would think, 'I can't do it the way he needs me to', 'What if I fail, like last time', 'He'll shout at me for being incompetent', 'He'll think I'm useless'.

At this stage, it would be easy for us to point the finger at his brother, suggesting he needs to change. Whilst that may well be true at one level, we have no right to change others, we can only work on ourselves.

We surfaced that at an early age, my client developed a low self-esteem due to the relationship with his aggressive father, influencing him specifically as the second sibling. Therefore, our focus was to re-landscape his garden by building a stronger view of his qualities, strengths and capabilities, gathering evidence that reinforced these views. Through diligent practice, he found that his reshaped self-beliefs influenced a completely different behaviour.

By changing his internal focus, there was a direct, external impact. Through his increased self-esteem, he was more confident in standing up for himself, he asked clarifying questions, negotiated for more time, asked for help and demonstrated a stronger presence. In response, his brother respected him more, treated him like an adult and became less demanding. Their relationship improved drastically, and all because of my client's change in his internal belief system.

This story shows how, when we change what we think, we can begin to alter our conditioned behaviour. We can challenge what we thought to be true, that actually show up as fallacies and delusions, often shaped around other's stories or dramas. We learn to create our own truths and based on those we are able to demonstrate more assertion.

If we want to develop assertive behaviours then we need to examine the quality of our internal self-worth. If we do not think we are worthy, then our external behaviours match this view of ourselves with timid body language, soft tone, low volume and avoidance behaviour.

When we believe in ourselves, our ability to speak out and confront issues alters drastically. Now we can begin to see the ingredients laid out before us like a recipe that creates a robust fruit cake. These then provide the basis for an authentic layer of icing that holds up firmly amidst life's challenges.

Fear's Role in our Non-assertion

I'd like to say a little something about fear and its role in our behaviour patterns. What is fear? Fear can be both an emotion and a thought induced instinctively when threatened by danger. When we believe something will harm us or threaten our happiness or security, fearful thoughts and feelings arise that paralyse our ability to act assertively.

Our primal fight and flight instincts kick in and produce protective behaviours that are not considered or rational. Fears are primal, deeply rooted in our conditioning and many people think that they cannot be cured because of that depth. For some this may be true, if this is their mind-set. Although, there are many different tools for eliminating or, at the very least, reducing the impact that fears have on our lives.

SID – Self-imposed Doubts

Before we leave this introductory chapter, there is just one more piece of information I would like to present - the concept of SID. I have found that creating an identity that encapsulates our negative thought patterns, has been incredibly helpful in their eventual elimination. By characterising our negativity, it lessens what can feel like a huge ocean of pessimism and can soften its effect on us. This makes it so much easier to work on than the overwhelming *to do* list.

There are several different characterisations used to brand our negativity; demons, thought gremlins; internal voice. I like the idea of SID – Self-imposed Doubts, as it defines this negative internal dialogue perfectly.

At this point, using our imagination, I would like us to create an image of SID that suits our purpose. Give him or her unappealing features that increases our loathing of the character. The more we associate pain, discomfort or disdain to SID, the easier it is for us to eliminate him/her. Having completed this, we can begin to identify the negative internal dialogue that plagues our conscious mind, taking us a long way to re-building our self-esteem and weeding our subconscious garden.

With some science and useful information behind us, we can move swiftly onto the magic that is reprogramming our subconscious mind.

Identifying your SIDs – Exercise

In the middle of a piece of paper, illustrate your SID character. Then allowing your mind to work freely, start to list the doubts, fears, anxieties and negative views you have of yourself.

They are likely to start with phrases like, 'I can't', 'I should/shouldn't', 'What if', 'I'm not', 'I haven't', 'I never/always', 'I'm unable to', 'It's impossible to', 'You can't', 'You are lazy/stupid, irritating, frustrating.', 'If only'.

Take as much time as you need for this exercise and think about all the phrases that you hear. They will be criticisms, personal attacks, disapprovals and judgements. It may feel like a hard exercise, although surfacing your SIDs will empower you to change these debilitating beliefs and free yourself from them.

Notice what comes up for you in terms of emotions. You may experience anything from sorrow, grief, sadness, anger or relief. Sometimes just being able to commit them to paper can be quite cathartic. Acknowledge all that you feel, deny nothing. We will be taking another step with this list shortly, so worry not, we shall return to these SIDs.

"FEAR – False Evidence Appearing Real"

Chapter 3
Reprogramming the Subconscious Mind

"The subconscious mind shapes 95% or more of our life experiences."

Joseph Murphy

The 1990's was the decade of the *power of positive thinking* revolution. The basic premise was that if we thought positively then we would achieve positive results. This was sound, in theory, although essentially flawed because neuroscience had not sufficiently verified the link between the conscious and subconscious mind. As we now recognise, our subconscious is critical to the experiences we attract, to the quality of our relationships and our self-image. So merely having a positive thought in our conscious mind is not enough to change our deeply engrained programmes, which continue to run the show. We need a more robust strategy to ensure that we re-landscape our garden and project a more sustained and assertive presentation.

This next chapter focuses on how we can move beyond the simplicity of positive thinking, into a new realm of re-tuning strategies that offer us the opportunity to rewrite out-dated programmes that no longer serve us.

Power of Mind over Matter

Armed with some powerful knowledge about our brain and mind, we can begin to consider the interesting possibility that we can change our old beliefs. By actively making new choices about what we think and embedding those thoughts into new beliefs, we can begin to create a more fulfilled future. Let's just recap on the key points:

- Our subconscious mind runs the show and holds all our hard-wired programmes, conditions and beliefs. It does not judge, rationalise or ponder – it reflexively responds based on the programmes implanted into it.

- Repeated events, other people's stories, messages and language we hear, create our subconscious landscape through which we experience the world.

- When the mind is engaged in consistently negative thoughts, it has a chemical, physical and behavioural impact on us.

- Every belief and conditioned programme has been learned through repeated assimilation and so we therefore have the capacity to learn new beliefs and conditions.

- Our conscious mind is a creative source that plans, rationalises and holds all our thoughts.

- Our conscious mind sits in the pre-frontal cortex, which is responsible for observing, self-reflecting, evaluating and planning.

- Thoughts, beliefs and ideas we hold about ourselves or that we have been taught are the basis for our self-worth and are planted into our subconscious.

- The interdependent relationship between our subconscious and conscious mind is hugely powerful and must be acknowledged and channelled if we are to truly succeed.

- Positive thinking alone will not work, long-term. We need to recognise the power of our subconscious mind, its malleability and its openness to autosuggestion.

As we discussed in the last chapter, neuroscience is presenting revelations all the time and the latest research on the *placebo effect* is shining a new light on how the brain works.

Bruce Lipton states;

"..some people get better when they believe (falsely) they are getting medicine. When patients get better by ingesting a sugar pill, medicine defines it as the placebo effect."

The bottom line to this is that whatever we believe or perceive, whether true or false, has a chemical and physical impact on our behaviour patterns. In her article, *Mind over Matter*, Dr Lissa Rankin describes a patient who was receiving Radiotherapy to shrink a tumour. After an X-ray to assess the results, they found the tumour had indeed shrunk, although doctors discovered the equipment had been faulty and had not administered the treatment. The effectiveness of the patient's mind to believe in the treatment was powerful enough to create a physical change in their condition.

On its own, we could say that was just co-incidence or chance, although more and more clinical studies are showing the placebo effect. If we believe that something works, then our mind's mechanics is chemically driven by those thoughts and transmit messages through our neural network, physically altering the 'state' of the condition without direct intervention.

This is, I acknowledge, a somewhat contentious issue, shaped by traditional medicine's belief system. Although given the emerging scientific data, I believe that for our assertive development purposes, this has some amazingly interesting possibilities.

Learning how to harness the power of our mind to achieve health, wealth, success and fulfilment is not just a fluffy concept conceived by life coaching gurus. It is a science, backed by hard data, which presents us with infinite possibilities, if we keep an open mind.

Exercising our Mental Muscle

It is said, "Use it or lose it", and how relevant this is to our brain's function. After all, it is a muscle, which we need to keep exercising.

Except we need to train it in the right way. Improper exercise gets us the wrong results and can cause harm and injury – just like our body's muscles. So, this is all about making sure we have the right type of workout to build our muscle in the right way. Here are some examples to experiment with.

The Balloon

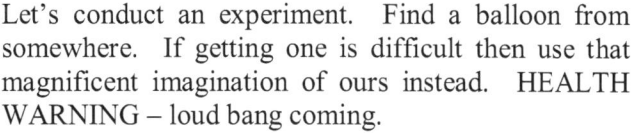

Let's conduct an experiment. Find a balloon from somewhere. If getting one is difficult then use that magnificent imagination of ours instead. HEALTH WARNING – loud bang coming.

Blow up the balloon for real or in our mind's eye and with a marker pen, write on one side a negative belief or SID we have about ourselves. On the other side of the balloon, draw a characterisation of SID. As we look at our balloon, this inflated view is what is taking up room in our conscious mind and is affecting our subconscious patterns.

Now with a sharp object carefully pop the balloon. Collect all the pieces that have flown across the room and look at the writing left behind on the balloon. What do we notice? Amazingly the writing is still readable and intact, although notice how minute it is. The inflated SID is now small and insignificant. What does this tell us?

What it tells me is that we blow up these negative thoughts about ourselves, increasing their size, ferocity and density and yet, in reality, they are paltry. Each time we have a negative thought, we blow up yet another balloon and expand its meaning, when in practical terms it is just a thought, which we can change.

A thought is a thought – nothing other than an atom of micro-electric energy. The minute we realise this it alters our mind-set and creates the space for a new way of thinking. Old habits can die.

Stilling the Chattering Mind

From the earlier exercise ***Observing the Mind,*** we may recognise just how many thoughts we have and start to understand their impact on us. If we can train the mind to become still, then imagine how much more effective we could be.

Meditation is increasingly hitting our screens these days. No longer exclusively associated with New Age hippies, meditation is a scientific-based practice that gets great results and is now becoming an accepted part of modern, western life.

Investing just ten minutes a day to be still, concentrating the mind on our breath, allowing thoughts to arise and fall away can bring us a great sense of calm. Whilst we return to the active thinking that is required for our daily activities, we carry them out from a more peaceful place. Of course, we can return to that serene place anytime we need, especially if we have a difficult situation to handle such as a saying 'no', negotiating or asking for help. Taking a few moments to be still puts us in a much more constructive and less fearful place, allowing us to operate more productively.

A friend and colleague recently told me about a way he creates stillness and clarity, which I thought was a great technique. He regularly checks in with himself by asking, ***"How am I feeling right now?"*** He acknowledges that feeling, be it sadness, anger, frustration or fear and then asks, ***"What action do I need to take?"*** He will be very clear through his stillness what to do or not do next – sometimes just purely acknowledging how we feel in this present moment is enough, action is not always required.

Using constructive questioning techniques and meditation can really help still our busy mind and enable us to deconstruct and remove the chatter, allowing us to handle what is most important.

Positive Daily Journal

If we have a propensity to negative thinking, then we need to shift our focus to a more positive mind-set. Building up a positive muscle is important in creating a more assertive outlook on life and here is a technique to help.

Before you go to sleep, write down in a journal, all the good, positive or uplifting things that you have appreciated in your day. This may be as simple as hearing the Dawn Chorus, someone smiling at you, getting some nice feedback or watching the setting sun. Committing these events to paper is a great way to shift your mind from negative to positive.

Practise this for at least thirty days, as it helps you to see the good in things more naturally and, over time, retrain your mind.

Re-calibrating our Negative Thoughts

We have a number of different strategies to use that enable us to re-programme our subconscious patterns, resulting in a more efficient hard-drive. Now we know how malleable our subconscious mind is, we can use the philosophy of autosuggestion to develop our self-esteem.

In this section, I would like to share a couple of processes I use for my own development and in a professional capacity that achieve great results. It combines the well-documented science of affirmations, mind/body principles and mental muscle techniques.

Thanks to inspirational authors that I have had the privilege to read, I have developed my own process that has proved to diminish SID and increase self-esteem.

Building self-respect

At the heart of changing our limiting beliefs is our ability to develop a sense of self-value. If we learn how to endorse ourselves, then our approval seeking behaviour changes and we no longer look for external validation.

When you no longer rely on other's opinion of you to give you internal validation, then you begin to strengthen your self-esteem.

As Lynda Field suggests in her book, *Creating Self-Esteem*, self-validation is the key to change. The more we can learn to value ourselves the less SID can interfere with our success. The more we affirm our own value, the greater our achievements because we are driven by completely different motives.

I Am Exercise

Here is an exercise you can use to build up that all-important self-respect. Using a flower analogy, build up petals around the, *I AM core* by acknowledging your strengths and capabilities.

Petals might consist of:

I am: a strong leader, kind, sensitive to others, a good listener, supportive, a great coach

The idea behind this is that it shows our current magnificence and focuses our mind on all we already have and do rather than concentrating on what we can't do. This is such a powerful exercise and reminds our subconscious mind about our capabilities rather than our failings, thereby increasing our self-respect.

Refer to this daily and keep repeating and acknowledging your capabilities and strengths, and you will soon see the impact that this exercise can have on your self-esteem.

85

The Art of Forgiveness

To build a strong self-esteem, we may need to look backwards at events, people or situations that contributed to our lack of worthiness. When exploring the causes or sources, it is vital to remember that we are not looking for blame, either in ourselves or in others. It is about identifying, forgiving and accepting what has been. To blame, be angry or judge is the wrong mind-set to operate from and instead we must work at this with compassion and understanding.

Allowing ourselves the capacity to forgive someone is a highly empowering action that can change our stance from *victim of circumstance* to a *victor of our future*. By releasing the power that some past event or person may have over us is to give ourselves permission to live out a different, more fulfilling life.

Seven Steps to Higher Self-esteem – Banishing SID

Having characterised earlier the negative internal dialogue that lurks within our subconscious garden, (disguised as weeds), we are ready to use our conscious capability to take control. With the help of Bruce Lipton, Tony Robbins et al, I have developed a process that dismantles our negative thought patterns and helps create more positive internal dialogue.

To help work through banishing your SIDs, I suggest that you give yourself plenty of time working through each of these stages in a systematic way for the best results, rather than rushing through to the final step.

1.   Identify your Fears, SIDs and Negative Thought Patterns

Reconnect with the exercises in Chapter 2, where I asked you to notice your thoughts, fears and SIDs. For this process, I would like you to select just **three** that are most debilitating to you right now. You may have more than this, although once you are used to the process you can apply the same strategy to your other weeds.

Examples you may have on your list could be:

Nobody likes me.   *I always let people down.*

I'm scared of failing.   *I'll never amount to anything.*

2.   Creating Table Tops

In his book, *Awaken the Giant Within*, Tony Robbins uses a TABLE concept to represent our beliefs. The legs, which provide the table's stability, characterise the reference points that give our beliefs their certainty. Without legs, the table cannot stand and it has no definition.

So with this in mind, write down your three negative thought patterns and draw a box around them. Now begin thinking about evidence, experiences and reference points that will form your table's legs, which make your beliefs feel certain for you.

For example, my SID table top, **I always let people down**, may have the following evidence.

I remember missing a meeting because I hadn't checked my diary.

I was too ill to run a course, so I had to postpone the workshop.

Having considered your reference points, (your table's legs), you need to assess how strong they are. Looking at my first leg - my missed meeting was in fact over twenty years ago and the meeting still went ahead without me. With this challenge, I can begin to question how valid this leg is in holding up my belief. When I rationally scrutinise the evidence, it is just a fragile, pine leg based on two factors:

- Notice how far back I had to go to find a reference point.
- How little I actually let them down, in reality.

My second reference point was illness. I'm sure having to cancel the course was disappointing to the group, although the illness was out of my control and the course was rescheduled. So once again, this evidence really has very little substance and forms another weak leg.

Interestingly, I could only find those two examples. So, when I look at my table's composition it is unstable with only two weak legs holding it up. So, I have been able to collapse the belief because there are insufficient legs to support it and the two that exist are simply too weak.

Collapsing the belief is what we are aiming for. The more we weaken our perceived certainty, the easier it is to collapse it and strip away its power over us. Some pointers to remember about finding table legs:

• Legs that are distant recollections can be less powerful than recent examples.	• Even three legs make a table unstable if they are not positioned correctly.
• If evidence is based on 'Someone told me', focus on the fact that only one person told you, not ten.	• Words like *always* and *never*, need an equivalent number of examples, so insufficient evidence weakens the belief.
• Even if one of your legs feels true, you still need three more for the table to stand strong.	• Legs may have some truth for you, although if even one of them has a weakness then the table wobbles.
• Taking too much time to think about legs indicates a weakness of the belief, as you are finding it hard to justify it.	• If legs are bowed, made of pine or have splinters of doubt, then they are weak. Strong legs are made of oak.

3. Collapsing the Table

Having made positive in-roads in collapsing, or at the very least destabilising the table, we now have the scope to see the unfounded truth upon which we have based our belief. With that possibility in mind, we begin to disempower it even further, using autosuggestion.

Return to your three table tops, which I hope have now started to wobble. For each box, I would like you to put a cross through each one and write the word DELETED. This signals to the brain that this programme no longer has a role to play in our subconscious. At the top of the page, also add, I AM CHOSING TO DELETE THESE SIDs.

4. Reframing our Beliefs

Having collapsed and deleted the three negative beliefs, we have some space. That space needs to be filled with positive tables that, when consistently implanted begin to cultivate a greater self-worth.

Using those three deleted beliefs, we now need to reframe them so that they adopt a positive angle. Taking my example, we could change:

I always let people down.	To	**I am conscientious.**
Nobody likes me.	To	**I am loved and lovable.**
I am scared of failing.	To	**I learn from my mistakes.**
I'll never succeed.	To	**I focus on being the best I can be.**

Language, as we have already seen, plays such a delicate role in how we feel about ourselves and how we behave. It is, therefore, vital to choose the right language that empowers not weakens. Here are the phrases I recommend to replace old, out-dated and untrue beliefs:

I can	*I am*	*I have (already)*	*I focus on*	*I commit to*
I am learning to	*I acknowledge*	*I am becoming*	*I am able to*	*I am capable of*

When we use these phrases, we are sending out a strong message for our subconscious mind to receive and, through repetition, it quickly adopts new programmes and conditions. So rewrite your three SIDs into positive phrases that feel good to you.

5.   New Table Tops and Legs

Having acquired some better sounding phrases, now we need to construct them into solid tables. In the same way, negative beliefs become certain for us through reference points, so our new, reframed beliefs also need that same certainty. It is this formula, which sets apart the *positive thinking* revolution to the p*ower of the mind* philosophy.

Armed with your three reframed phrases, draw a box around them to represent table tops and now develop four sturdy legs, characterised by evidence that stabilises their truth for you. Here are my table tops:

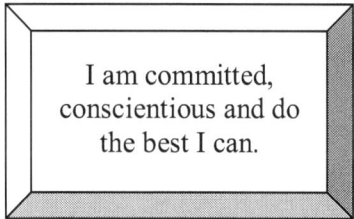

I am committed, conscientious and do the best I can.

My four legs are:

- I enjoy meeting people's needs and making them happy
- I am receptive to people's needs through my listening skills and intuition
- I have history of a hard work ethic and feedback to support this from clients
- I am an assertive communicator, which enables me to say what I am able to achieve.

Notice here that the four reference points focus on my abilities and skills to support this belief. Here's another example:

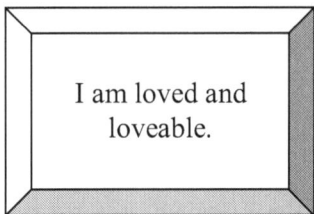

I am loved and
loveable.

- My family show and tell me how much they love me.
- A new group that I have recently joined show warmth towards me and have given me positive feedback about how I come across.
- I have a huge capacity to love others and this comes back to me in return.
- I have life-long friends who tell me how much they value me.

Notice how these legs are specific pieces of evidence that contribute towards validating and strengthening my belief – I have not made them up. They are real experiences that stabilise my new thought and I know it to be true. They ensure that no SID interference can threaten my new belief from taking hold.

6. The Written Word is More Powerful

Having played around with our new thoughts and attached evidence to them, we now need to remind ourselves of them every day. So, write them down and keep them visible, perhaps on the fridge, in your car somewhere or in your wallet or a drawer at work. When we commit something to writing it has a stronger emotional and mental resonance with us, so be prepared to put your new thoughts out there.

7. Repetition

"Repetition is the Mother of Skill."

The more we repeatedly do something or say something, the more likely we are to master it. We know this to be true at so many levels. Think about learning to drive a car, playing golf or some other sport. We only became competent through making mistakes, learning and repeating the techniques until it became second nature.

Inspired by NASA's research into the effect weightlessness had on astronauts, data demonstrates that new habits are created in around thirty days. So, this final stage of the process follows the same principle. When we repeat *new ways* consistently for thirty days, our brain develops new neural pathways and our habits change. Learn to practise our new statements last thing at night just as we settle down to sleep and again as soon as we wake up. These are highly receptive times for our subconscious mind. The more we repeat them, the more our brain embeds the neural pathways and the more substantial our new hardwiring becomes.

I encourage you to follow this process for your three SIDs and then over the next **thirty days**, consistently repeat your new beliefs. Notice what interference comes up from SID and write this down. This may be either another negative belief that needs tabling or simply highlighting some of the wording that is not working for you. Adjust it and keep repeating.

I had a client recently who committed to this process and one of her goals was to write down experiences that were 'great'. She really struggled with this and gave up after a couple of weeks. At our next session, she shared this with me, realising that it was just not a word in her vocabulary and each time she wrote down something 'great', she received a whole heap of interference that inhibited her practice.

We explored the words that were more comfortable for her and she settled on 'positive' and 'good'. This enabled her to move forward with the mental workout that she knew she needed to do.

Science of Affirmations

In conjunction with the positive thinking revolution, came the introduction of affirmations. Big names like Louise L. Hay and Tony Robbins, talk about the role affirmations play in helping our self-esteem grow. Despite some scepticism, their continued existence owes itself to, what some people might call the New Age movement. Yet they are so much more than that thanks to the efforts of physicists, chemists and biologists who continue to present the science behind our mind, thoughts and affirmations.

When we apply science to the techniques I have recommended, then our sceptical ego is removed from the equation and we are left focusing on improving our self-esteem and respect. Here's a list that captures the essence of affirmations:

- A thought is just a thought and it can be changed and challenged.

- What we put our attention to, grows.

- A positive thought can turn into a positive belief through repetition in the same way that negative conditions were created by something we learned and observed in childhood.

- Our ability to learn and adapt is innate and, irrespective of our age, we can learn new ways of thinking and behaving. With the right programming and practise, we can change our self-criticism into self-appreciation.

- Thoughts only have power when we add meaning to them.

- Our conscious mind has the ability to choose and so we can choose to have a positive mind-set and self-belief.

- The more evidence we have of something being true, the more meaning we attach to it and the greater is our belief in it.

- When we experience something joyful or happy, we release different chemicals in the body that produces a feel-good factor. If this is true of experience then it can be true of positive and appreciative thoughts and mind-sets.

- Studies highlighting the effects of twenty minutes meditation each day show how stress can reduce by 50%. If a calm mind can create this change in physiology then imagine the impact affirmations can have.

- *Placebo effect* studies have shown that it works when patients **desire** to be well, **expect** to be well and **believe** that they will be well. When we apply the same three ingredients to changing our thoughts with affirmations, then we can have the same remarkable effects on our self-esteem.

- When we combine a visual image with an affirmation, we affect specific neurons in the brain that, when it magnifies, creates new, neural pathways.

- We know that certain music creates our mood, either uplifting us or inducing feelings of sadness. A musical tone or a song's words affect us chemically and so if we practise applying positive, uplifting and appreciative thoughts towards our self and others, we can influence a chemical change to our mood.

- The meaning behind words activates thoughts, feelings and mental images. Therefore, if we use positive words, it triggers a cycle of healthier thoughts, feelings and ultimately behaviours.

- Words affect us at two levels; through our interpretation of their meaning and through their tonality. Words and phrases take on a completely new significance when they are positive.

- Through repetition, neural pathways develop in our brain. Affirmations can, therefore form new tracks for us to play that, through consistent application, become new habits.

- Affirmations are a form of constructive auto-suggestive reconditioning.

- Whatever the conscious mind assumes to be true authorises our subconscious mind to draw specific conclusions towards a problem or situation that we are facing.

With these pointers summarised, I hope it embeds the logic and science that is behind positive thinking, affirmations and reprogramming our subconscious mind. With confidence in the process and the knowledge, we are now able to add a degree of faith to the matter and with it, a real solution to low self-esteem. Here's how we create affirmations.

Five P's of Affirmations

Here are the five essential ingredients to writing robust affirmations:

Positive

Keep affirmations in the positive at all times, so:

This	Not This
I am committed to....	I am no longer going to…
I am getting slimmer.	I am losing weight.

Present Tense

Avoid conditional tenses such as ought, should and could as they leave a margin for error. Avoid future tense, as again it leaves room for excuses and procrastination. It must be in the NOW.

This	Not This
I am successful.	I will be successful.
	I could be successful.

Personal

They must be about you, so phrased in the first person. Avoid the third or objective person.

This	Not This
I am, I can, I have	We are going to… It is going to be…

Powerful

The affirmation must have strength behind it to recondition an old pattern. So ensure you select a statement that gives you confidence, belief and meaning.

This	Not This
I am committed to thinking, feeling and behaving more positively.	I can be a positive thinker.

Proved

Anchor affirmations by either adding **concrete actions** or **robust evidence** to secure the thought as a belief. It keeps any interference and doubt at bay.

This	Not This
I am committed to thinking, feeling and behaving more positively. • I repeat my affirmations three times a day • I challenge negative thoughts and replace them with positive statements • I have received comments from my colleagues that I seem more positive.	I am committed to thinking, feeling and behaving positively.

Having done this exercise and achieved a successful shift, you will be ready to tackle other negative thought patterns that you have identified. Revisit the rest of the list and follow exactly the same process for each one and you will be well on your way to greater self-esteem. I know, because I have committed to exactly the same process and it has and still is working for me.

One final thought. It may seem as though this section has been about ridding ourselves of the bad and replacing with the good. Well to some degree, this is true. Although a point to remember - we are a blend of shadow and light, good and not so good.

We must acknowledge the less healthy aspects of ourselves and embrace them, as by fighting, we only end up with further resistance. When we honour the bad feelings, the negative thoughts, fears and judgements we make of others, then with compassion, we give ourselves the permission to refocus our efforts on the positives.

We are and will always be *both* not *either/or*. When we realise this, we can choose where to place our power and utilise our strength in the best way. When we feel down, we must acknowledge it, explore it and resolve it, if we can. The key is not staying with that emotion or thought. When we do, it starts to take root and could become an unhealthy pattern that changes the way we behave.

This chapter has focused on how to re-write our subconscious programmes so we can alter our behaviour patterns. With a stronger self-respect, we have a more robust self-esteem, which changes the intentions behind our behaviours and allows us to act with integrity.

The next chapter shifts our attention from the inside conversations we have with ourselves, to the way we interact with others. Communication is everything, as we are already beginning to realise.

"Thoughts are the starting point of all change and so the source of all change is within you." Dr David R. Hamilton PhD

Chapter 4
Interactive Dialogue

"Communication is the response you get, regardless of the intention. If you get the wrong response, then change your communication."

Definition of communication

Every relationship needs it, families rely on it and partnerships demand it – communication is at the heart of everything.

We started this section acknowledging that there are two distinct types of communication; the one in our heads - our internal dialogue and the external one we use to interact with others. To me, communication is at the root of everything. It is so critical for us to get it right, and now we have some tools to master our mental chatter.

The principles behind our *interactive dialogue* are similar, although there are some more detailed considerations that I would like to offer in this chapter. Hundreds of books have been published that focus on *the art of communication,* yet many of them present a one-dimensional perspective. I believe we must deliver more than a transactional communication – for me it is all about how we *interact* that counts and the two are very different.

We will be looking at how to create interactive, meaningful and influential conversations that position us assertively, enabling us to generate positive outcomes, relationships and resolutions.

Self-esteem and Interactive Dialogue

We have already seen that if our internal dialogue constantly invalidates us, this affects the messages we send from our brain to our body, influencing us at a physiological level. Our body language subtly mirrors our self-perception, which then reflects through our behaviours, dialogue and interactions.

Our unconscious display to others releases a subtle energy that people around us pick up. This shapes their response to us – which can then invalidate us further, eroding our confidence and reinforcing our low self-esteem. When we feel more positive about ourselves we project this unknowingly, and it influences our language and presence, to which others respond.

We may be familiar with the idea that if someone in our household starts the day in a bad mood, how quickly it spreads to others. How we present ourselves influences other's energy at a subtle and unconscious level and so stresses the importance of working from the inside out. Get our inside healthy and what we project becomes more assertive, natural and authentic.

A New Model of Communication

If we delve into the old communication ideal, it talks about having a two-way conversation, listening actively and planning what you say to achieve a positive outcome.

Superficially, there is nothing wrong with this model, although the latest opinion about the art of success focuses more on **how** we engage with people. It is a much more profound *model of interaction* that creates greater meaning and heart-felt communication. When we team this up with Emotional Intelligence, Neuro-linguistic Programming and Conscious Communication, then we have the ingredients for assertive interactions.

Add to this the amount of conversations conducted remotely via Skype, emails and telephones, it is no wonder that this topic keeps raising its head in every personal development manual. This **Interactive Dialogue** model below, summaries that sophistication:

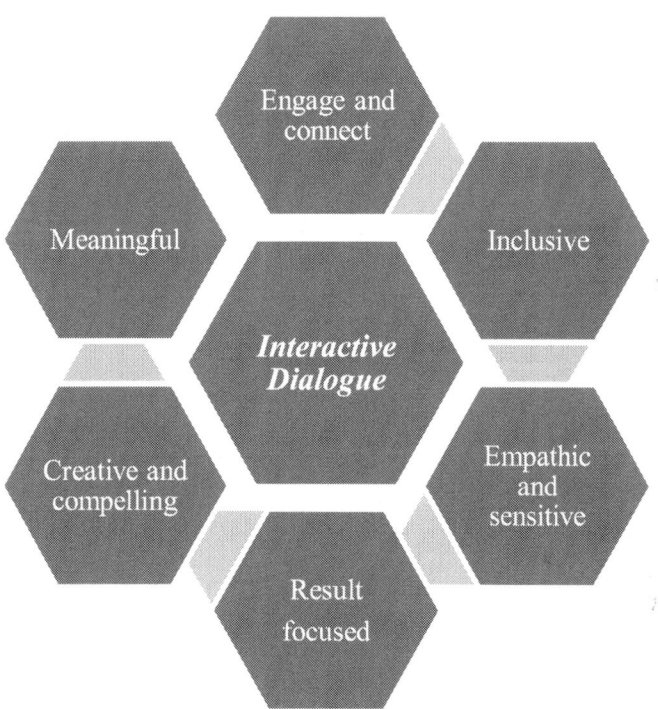

This more engaging approach to communication is now at the heart of fulfilling relationships and personal assertiveness.

Engaging Interactions – The Way Forward

The minute we take responsibility for our part in interactions and relationships, is the moment things begin to change. All the time we blame others or events for the *state* of our association, the more we get stuck in a blame, resentment, frustration cycle that exaccerbates our negative experience.

When we realise that what we do and say impacts on others, we immediately take control of the reins and start driving our interaction forward. Notice how a simple smile can change the dynamic between two people. This is the influence we have when we become aware and take responsibility.

That responsibility invites us to focus on the Interactive Dialogue model and, having changed our internal chatter, gives us the opportunity to invest thought into how we come across to others.

Engaging, Empathic and Meaningful Interactions

The distinction between *communication* and *interaction* is that it encourages a different level of inclusion, awareness and sensitivity. When we begin to interact with others by experiencing the world through their eyes, we are a step closer to building a more fulfilling rapport with them.

Whilst coaching one of my clients, she described having difficulties with her aggressive partner who generated a defensive reaction in her. I encouraged her to step inside his shoes and experience what his world might look and sound like. Now whilst we could only surmise what had influenced his behaviour, the opportunity to learn and understand was enough to shift my client's defensiveness. She came to appreciate that past events were likely to have influenced his patterns and that he may be concealing a low self-esteem. She acknowledged that her responsibility was to shift the dynamic of their relationship by adopting a more empathic approach.

Three months later, she reported that their relationship had changed significantly, because she was choosing to behave more assertively and be more appreciative. Reducing her defence mechanism enabled the energy of the situation to shift, allowing them to operate at a more constructive level.

We can classify effective interactions by our ability to see through another's eyes and communicate in such a way that it appeals to and engages them. If we drive our communication only by our intention and agenda, then we miss the opportunity to create accord. Taking time to see things from another's perspective is hugely powerful and enables us to adjust what we say and how we say it, to achieve the best outcome for us both – an assertive resolution.

What does that mean we need to do? Here are three recommendations:

Engaging	Empathic	Meaningful
•Connect by getting to know people. •Involve them. •Actively listen. •Ask open questions. •Talk **with** not **to** them. •Look at them, not stare. •Smile. •Acknowledge their views. •Adapt your style to suit their needs	•See the world through their eyes, not your own. •Take time to understand their perspective. •Use, 'I agree', 'I understand', and 'I appreciate'. •Be considerate. •Be compassionate. •Honour their views •Show you value them by actively listening.	•Talk so they understand. •Match your energy to theirs. •Speak their language. •Work out how they like to hear things. •Learn their motivations and values. •Become more people-centred than task-focused. •Be clear and transparent.

Be Outcome Focused

As author, Stephen Covey once said,

"Start with the end in mind".

In most cases, for an interaction to be productive, it needs to have an outcome, an end-point to which we must head. If we are unclear about what action or result we want from our communication, then ambiguity, lack of focus and misunderstandings occur.

Before we enter into any conversation, it's really helpful if we think about what we want to achieve from it. Now it's not always easy to do, although if we can think about it beforehand, it will help the flow of the conversation, for example:

- **A work meeting** – what do we need to present, inform or gather from the agenda?

- **A difficult discussion** – what feedback or message do we need to give and is there a particular behaviour that needs to change?

- **Asking for help** – what do we specifically need help with and from whom?

- **Giving instructions** – what specific task does someone need to do for us and by when?

- **A negotiation** – what result do we want from our discussion, and where are we prepared to compromise?

- **Resolving problems** – being clear what the issues or challenges are and who is best placed to help resolve it.

- **Complaint handling** – if we need to complain about service we have or are receiving, we need to be clear what the issue is and what we wish to happen as a result of our complaint.

Each interaction is unique, because the recipient has their own personal view of the world, shaped by their experiences. We can never plan for

103

every eventuality, although it is more about the intention we put into the interaction.

Where there is an interaction that has specific significance, value or importance (as opposed to just a chat over coffee or a catch up), then invest time in thinking about this, as a smoother transition is ensured and, most likely, a constructive and positive outcome experienced.

The Who and What are Sorted – Now for the How

Frank Carson, a Belfast comedian once said,

"It's the way I tell 'em".

A joke delivered with the wrong emphasis, tone, confidence or body language can turn it into a damp squib. If we deliver our message inappropriately, it leaves no end of damage and confusion.

An airline pilot often takes a different approach on landing at an airport because of the changing conditions. The same is true for us when we interact. The environment surrounding our interactions is always shifting and whilst our style might remain the same, our approach must be appropriate to the recipient, our message and what we want to achieve. No two interactions will ever be the same, especially given the numerous communication vehicles available to us.

The important thing to remember is that we must always start our interactions from the space of our audience and the message we need to deliver. Email may just be too impersonal or face to face simply impractical. A word of caution! Watch out for SID's interplay with the selection. There may be a difficult interaction to have and we decide that to email or phone rather than face the person is easiest. Easiest is not necessarily the best and our *fear of confrontation* or our *need to be liked* must be addressed if we are going to interact appropriately and assertively.

Having selected our option, we now need to turn our interaction into something inspiring, compelling, inclusive and collaborative. These are,

I believe, what turns our communication into something more meaningful. Here are some ideas on how to do that.

Be compelling and inspire action
- Get into recipients' hearts and minds.
- Tailor your message to meet their needs.
- Hook them into your message with rich vocab.
- Identify what matters to them.
- Convey what is in it for them.

Inclusive
- Ask for people's views and opinions.
- Ask open questions to get them involved.
- Invite input of ideas, suggestions and options.
- Use words like we, together, us and how, when, what, as often as you can.

Interaction Nuances

I often find myself thinking that with technological advances, the art of person to person communication is dying and it is seen as being easier to text someone rather than pick up the phone and have a simple chat. We might consider that the need to connect is just not necessary these days. Although if we are parents, we need to connect; if we have neighbours we need to build relationships; if we are part of a community, we need to engage and at work, of course, how we communicate is key to standing out amongst our colleagues. With the blend of empathy, assertion, creativity and enthusiasm, we can demonstrate so many qualities that technology is starving us of.

With these thoughts in mind, here are some interaction nuances that can set us apart from others:

Neuro-linguistic Programming

NLP has been around for over four decades heralding a powerful discipline, which we can all access, enabling us to build influential relationships and develop inner confidence. NLP promotes itself as the premier psychological model of positive communication and personal success.

Its loose translation is about how:

- To understand how the brain works, (the neuro)
- The language we use affects us and our interaction with others, (the linguistics)
- We decode this partnership into meaningful behaviours and actions that guide us towards successful outcomes, (the programming).

When we become aware of the interplay between this trio, we arm ourselves with a series of strategies that provide us with opportunities to live and work more effectively with others.

Yet again, NLP deserves a book all of its own, although in this section I aim to summarise the most relevant features that assist our interactive dialogue.

The premise to NLP is a ***fascination with people***, how their thoughts and their behaviours work. When we make the transition from being task-centred to people-focused, we make a crucial shift in mind-set.

By inspiring others we create an energy that encourages tasks to be completed effortlessly, people to be delighted consistently and teams to operate optimally, because they are appreciated, involved and understood.

Entwined with this philosophy is understanding how values, beliefs, thoughts and language interact, both for the individual and amongst a group. When we notice how our own view of the world interplays with others, we begin to see how relationships evolve and how we can have a positive bearing on them.

Some key NLP features that are worth noting, within the context of our interactive dialogue discussions are:

- **Observing, attending and listening**

  When we invest in watching what people do, how they do it and why they do it, we immediately access valuable information that helps get the best from our relationship.

- **Making conscious choices about our interactions**

  Having observed and considered, we can then make choices about how best to interact, so that all parties achieve a win-win outcome. Subtleties such as tone, body language, words, pace, can all be ingredients to a successful interaction outcome.

- **Building rapport and empathy**

  Every moment of our interaction must drive towards the desire to build rapport, empathy and, ultimately trust. With these in place, our relationships will go from strength to strength.

- **Be respectful**

  Respect is at the heart of any relationship and we can only build rapport when respect is our partner. Learning to appreciate other's views and perspectives is vital – this does not mean we have to agree, we just need to be respectful of another's right to their opinions.

- **Match and mirror**

  In the 1960s, William Condon coined the phrase *Cultural Micro-rhythms,* which discussed the unconscious dance and rhythm we engage in when in rapport with someone.

  When we match someone's posture, tone, pace and even language, at a subtle level, they feel valued. Mirroring has the same premise; we just reflect back their cues, again creating a sense of affiliation. This is not intended as a manipulative or orchestrated technique. Just finding subtle ways to adjust our posture, match our language and generate the same energy as our recipient, signals a subconscious acceptance between us and helps build a stronger connection.

- **We communicate with our whole body**

  Whilst *thinking* happens in our conscious minds, the effects of those thoughts transmit through every fibre of our being. Thoughts translate into emotions, emotions colour our language and tone of voice and these vibrate through our body posture and gestures.

  Learning to hear what someone is saying without having to speak is an art, although once we are attuned to what someone is saying with their bodies, not just their words, then we have an amazing tool, enabling us to adjust to their experiences of the world and build trust, rapport and quality interactions.

When we hone these techniques, then the results we can achieve from our conversations improve and so too do the depth of our relationships.

Questions are the Answer

As a coach and facilitator, I have learned the power of questioning. One question, the right question can turn someone's confusion into clarity and change their whole way of thinking.

I love this quote from Joseph O'Connor and Andrea Lages in their book *Coaching with NLP*,

"Questions are like spotlights that shine into dark places".

This really gets to the heart of the role questions have in our interactions. We can be trapped too often into thinking that talking gets us the results we need, especially when pressurised. Alas that's really only half the story and 50% of the potential. When we ask a question, we open up the gap between two people, inviting interaction, debate and the sharing of information. Without questions we simply resort to telling, instructing and dictating, which is not transformative in nature.

Questions are engaging, involving, inviting, explorative, provocative and reflective. When asked with the right intent, it can change the whole dynamic of an interaction. Sometimes just the simplicity of asking: *"What do you think?"* can send a wave of inclusivity that alters our joint experience of that interaction.

Tips for great, powerful questions:

- Keep it Simple Speaker (KISS)

- Keep them open – who, what, when, why, where and how, with **what** and **how** being the most powerful.

- Keep them sensory - What do you think, feel, know? How do you feel? How do you see this working out? How does this sound to you?

- Time your questions appropriately.

- Once asked, keep quiet and listen. A question asked that is not heard is no question at all.

- Keep them succinct – multi-layered questions are unhelpful and confusing.

- Ask questions that put the recipient in a positive state, such as, 'What is the best thing that could happen here?' 'What skills do you have that could help?' 'What is the best-case scenario?'

Vocabulary of Success – Sensory-based words/phrases

Words have so much power that when we get them wrong, just notice the awkwardness around us. One word placed wrongly can spell disaster. Conversely, the right words can create magic, energy and win-win results.

From an NLP perspective, choosing the right words when we interact is critical to a positive outcome. Sensory-based words enable us to reflect back to our recipient language that matches with their subconscious preferences. These fall into three categories:

	Visual	Auditory	Kinaesthetic
Words	See, look, notice, observe, illustrate, imagine, outlook, perspective, reflect, show, visualise, watch, focus.	Ask, sound, hear, resonate, tell, tune, comment, question, remark, discuss.	Balance, contact, feel, seem, handle, stress, touch, sense.
Phrases	Imagine how this might work. We see eye to eye on this. Show me how. Beyond a shadow of a doubt. See this in your mind's eye. Shed some light on this for me.	How does that sound to you? That resonates. In a manner of speaking. We're on the same wavelength. Music to my ears. I hear what you're saying.	I can't put my finger on it. How does that feel? On balance, which is best? I feel it in my bones. Hang on a minute.

The art of successful sensory-based vocabulary is to first listen to what people are telling us, pick up the words they are using and then match our response to them. We then start building a powerful rapport with them and they feel valued.

Vocabulary of Success – Influential language

As Confucius said,

> **"Without knowing the force of words, it is impossible to know men."**

It has to be worth investing just a little time in looking at other words and phrases that either enhance or weaken our interactions. The more conscious we are of our language, the greater the chance of positive results. Here is a list of words and phrases to consider:

	Powerless	Influential
Words	You, us, them, possibly, may be, try, perhaps, should, nice, ought, fine, difficulty, but, problem, fearful, might, just, always, never, everything, only, fault, hopefully, sort of, hope, but, wish, however.	**I, we, together, commit, great, amazing, learning, challenge, and, intrigued, curious, potential exploratory, can, have, inspired, driven, motivated, feel, believe, sometimes, often, will, ownership, responsibility, accountability.**
Phrases	I can't. I should/ought. What if? To be honest/truthful/fair. It's only me. I tend to think. I'm sorry. I could be mistaken, but… If it's not too much trouble.	**I need/must.** **How might it work out?** **I would prefer/I could.** **I am/I do/I can/I have.** **I apologise.** **I accept/I choose.** **I agree/I appreciate/I understand.** **I feel X when Y happens.** **I can't now, maybe later.**

We must choose our vocabulary wisely, as our choices affect our internal state, our external demeanour and the energy of the people around us.

I ran an Assertiveness seminar for a group of thirty Shipping Administrators and we had a very engaging and buoyant time together.

Towards the end of the day, I carried out a vocabulary experiment to show them the impact our language can have on our physical being.

I split the room into two groups, giving each a set of cards with different words and phrases for them to discuss. I then asked them to face each other and describe their seminar experience.

The first group were highly animated about their learning, were visibly upbeat and most inspiring in their body language.

The second group talked in low-tones, came across in a lethargic way, using insipid language and offering very little inspiration about the day.

When I asked them to reveal the words on their cards, they were:

Sunflowers	Happy	Dark	Winter
Sunshine	Joyful	Empty	Depressed
Laughter	Peaceful	Cold	Alone
Beach	Spring	Sad	Isolated
New life	Smiles	Homeless	Bare
Friends	Warmth	Angry	Resentful
Together	Sharing	War	Misery
Birdsong	Singing	Tears	Stormy
Grass cuttings	Bluebells	Rain	Hurt
Butterflies	Winning	Argument	Hate

The collection of words were so powerful that despite their motivated state going into the exercise, after being with the cards for no more than a couple of minutes, the second group's condition altered completely. Imagine what impact language can have on others if this is what vocabulary can do to our behaviours.

The words we consistently choose affect our behaviours, our relationships and the results we achieve. How amazing to think that something so small and seemingly insignificant can have so much power. Words can empower or depress, choose carefully.

Presence and Projection

The final word on Interactive Dialogue is around the subtlties of how we present ourselves. I don't mean the orchestrated way in which we might prepare for an interview to make a good first impression. I mean in the day to day authenticity that shows up when we have a restored self-esteem and have *people* at the heart of what we do and say.

On the Leadership programme I ran, participants would question what the word *presence* meant so that they knew what they had to 'do'. Peversely, there is little that we can do. Presence is a charisma, a poise, an air of confidence that exudes when we operate with authenticity.

When we master an internal strength based on self-belief and self-respect, speak from the heart, interact through the eyes of others and act with integrity, we naturally project an appearance, which reflects that which is inside. Presence is the art of existing authentically.

These then are gifts that we receive when we have mastered the ideas from this book. We walk tall, we talk confidently, we look natural. This is not forced, this is an instinctive bi-product of solid self-worth, calmness and indisputable substance. People around us respond to the aura of confidence that we display and want to be around us and are happy to engage with us. If there was ever a goal for our well-being , this surely has to be it?

"Words are, of course, the most powerful drug used by mankind."

Rudyard Kipling

Chapter 5
Action Planning

"In everything, the ends well defined, are the secet of durable success."

Victor Cousins, Philosopher

As I suggested in the first part of this book, goal setting is really important at this stage of your journey. I have read many 'self-help' books along my path and many have uplifted me, perhaps even motivated me, although if they haven't inspired me to act or make a change, then my reading may be wasted.

Change comes about when we are inspired to doing, thinking or feeling something different. Although we must be proactive, courageous and initiate change otherwise our status quo remains the same.

I believe when there is enough desire to change, then this creates a momentum that needs no pressure, forcing or pushing. Desire creates an innate propulsion that carries us forward. Armed with a clear focus on what we want to be different, commitment to see it through and diligent application, we can turn our goals into reality.

Having read this second section, what do you feel determined to change and inspired to do differently? Thinking this question through is important if we really want to revel in the positive results awaiting us.

Six Steps to Making Change Happen

As I outlined at the end of the first section, following a process is important to capture our commitments, so please follow these steps, which I have summarised below. To remind yourself of the detail, of course return back to pages 55-58.

Step 1 – **Review your Learning** – what has stood out for you?

Step 2 – **Review your Goals** – do they need to change?

Step 3 – **Your Inspirations** – what are you inspired to do differently?

Step 4 – **Questions are the Answers**

       What: will you specifically do differently?

       Why: is this action important to you?

       How: will you approach achieving this action?

       When: will you do this, over what period?

       Who: will need to support you and who is involved?

       Where: will this goal take place? At home, work or socially?

Step 5 – Do and Review – Take action.

Step 6 – Commit to Paper

With a stronger self-esteem, a newly landscaped garden and a new appreciation for the power of the mind, you are ready to move further forwards towards your authentic assertion.

Once again, I encourage you to use the next **four to six weeks** to experiment, talk, journalise and reflect on what is going well and what still needs adjusting as you head towards the third and final instalment.

If this series is capturing you, then the final section will be the real icing on the cake. We focus on pulling together all the inside out learning I have encouraged in the first two sections and give you an opportunity to combine it all in the application of handling situations with authentic assertion.

Inspired by past-participants, clients' real life circumstances and my own personal experiences, I show you how to overcome assertive challenges. Using the foundation of self-awareness inspired by these first two sections, you will be in a strong position to apply the techniques and tools in the final edition to master your assertion.

"All we are and all we have are nothing if we don't believe in them."

Karen Davies, Coach

Part 3

Assertive Strategy Guide

Chapter 1
Introduction to the Finale

**"All is possible when we know the possibilities are within
one self. It is only ourselves that limit us."**

Gaye Pipe

The root and the route to authentic assertion is using my *inside-out* philosophy, inspired by Stephen R. Covey's book, *The 7 Habits of Highly Effective People*. We can only create sustained and authentic assertive patterns when we understand what holds us back and then find ways to resolve those issues.

The first section we covered some critical principles about how to raise our self-awareness, after which we gain a tremendous understanding of our current behaviours and what could be holding us back from that illusive assertive Utopia.

The second section, **Creating Unshakeable Self-Esteem** looked at conquering the art of assertive interactions by exploring how our *internal dialogue* influences our self-esteem and how, through our *external dialogue,* others experience and build relationships with us. We discovered the role our thoughts have on both our self-worth and behaviour patterns and we explored some of the latest research that reveals the mind/body connection. In addition, we uncovered how to have *meaningful conversations* enabling us to develop greater connections with those we love and ensure that our everyday interactions become more fulfilling exchanges.

This third and final section brings our journey together, creating an exciting climax to our assertive challenges, offering us tools that create a long-lasting change in our behaviour. Having read the first two sections, with a degree of knowledge, understanding and faith, we are ready to embrace new ways of thinking, feeling and acting and begin to experience new results that can bring us so much more peace in this crazy, crazy world.

Assertive Vision

There is a lot of talk in the Personal Development field about the Law of Attraction and how this is an important strategy for accelerating personal fulfilment. Quite simply this focuses on setting a clear image in our minds about **what we want**. Through regular reviews of this vision and stepping up our game, we can attract people, events and situations that guide us towards our dreams.

As we now combine all the assertive theory from the previous two sections, I believe that generating a clear vision of our assertion moving forward, is important. So this next exercise creates a very powerful success strategy using the Law of Attraction.

Buddha is reported as saying,

"Be the change that you wish to see in the world."

It is only after we understand what the change is that we want to bring into our lives and can visualise how it will make us feel, that we can step up and become it and experience the result of that change.

Assertive Attraction Exercise

Wherever you are sitting right now, take a breath and get comfortable. Be present in this moment and allow your worries and pressures to subside, just for a while. Give your mind permission to be still.

Now focus your mind on three-six months from now. Imagine yourself behaving assertively and complete these three statements;

When I am assertive,

a. **I am**
b. **I feel**
c. **I can**

Now visualise your answers and put them into your own personal mind movie. See yourself behaving confidently, feel the effects of your increased assertion, hear the sound of your voice and notice the impact you are having on others.

Amplify this movie. Make it larger, louder and more colourful. Feel it coming alive. Get a real sense of how you feel watching this image. Notice the pleasure, excitement, happiness, satisfaction that is happening for you right now. Tune into this feeling as this is the reality of your assertion.

Repeat this mind movie daily and as you experience more intense satisfaction, you begin to attract positive situations. In addition to this, as you begin to apply the learning from all three sections, you step up your actions in such a way that you head actively towards your vision.

Benefits of Authentic Assertion

Ok, so we have the vision in our minds, we are playing out our movie on a daily basis and generating positive feelings when we do. Here is a quick reminder about why this assertive projection is so important to us.

Authentic, sustained assertion has huge benefits for us. All too often we put our energy into pleasing or dominating others. Assertion allows us to put *us* firmly back into the space that we have the right to be in. No longer do we have to stand on the side-lines, tentatively wondering how and when we should make our presence known. Equally, we no longer need to position ourselves in the middle, looking for the power of the limelight to feel some sense of worthiness.

Having taken our *assertive development journey* over the course of the last two sections, we begin to see the limitless possibilities for our potential and, through the conscious choices we can now make, get positive resolutions to our issues. What's more, when we operate this assertive simplicity from a place of robust self-esteem – we stand in a place of certainty and self-respect.

These symbiotic elements combine together to give us health, peace, natural behaviour and an armoury to deal with every situation that life presents to us. Sleepless nights lessen, conflicts fade, achievements increase and relationships flow better. Sure there will be challenging times that test our resilience, although with these tools we can cope, resolve and overcome them all in a more efficient and self-protective way.

We must give a mention to the benefits that others receive from our new position of confidence. The energy we project from our new space creates an enthusiastic atmosphere that others pick up on. When we project confidence, we generate confidence in others. When we deal with people respectfully, they respect us in turn. When we stand up for ourselves, people stop pushing us around. When we judge less, others do not judge us. The whole experience of interacting with people changes the minute we become more comfortable in our own skin and like the reflection in the mirror.

When these two elements are working better, then just imagine how our health will be. When we operate from an unassertive stand-point, we constantly live in a *fight and flight* position. The hormone Cortisol races through our bodies, keeping our major organs and muscles in a state of alert, ensuring that we can take defensive action at any time. Stress, the common translation for this state, is so prevalent in today's society that we have come to accept this as part of life. It really doesn't have to be.

We have adapted to this fast-pace of life and so are more likely to put our bodies under strain, often unknowingly. Stress-related illnesses and disease are on the increase; £40 billion is spent on anxiety issues alone, which when combined with our processed and convenience-style diet is putting our health under immense pressure.

When we allow ourselves to take a more authentic path through life that honours ourselves and others in a more compassionate and loving way, then our bodies have the opportunity to recover. We can bring ourselves out of *fight and flight* and almost re-boot our internal system allowing us to start on a path to well-being, building our mental and physical health.

So, are there any reasons for not harnessing this amazing development? Over the years that I have posed this question, my participants and clients have struggled to see any downsides to learning the art of assertion. Most particularly, when people see that this art is within themselves and that ultimately we are looking to create personal expansion, then everyone benefits.

"Everything can change from here."

Karen Davies, Coach

Chapter 2
Assertiveness Synopsis

"When we are no longer able to change a situation, we are challenged to change ourselves."

Victor Frankl

My intention in writing this book was to invite you on a personal journey of exploration that guides you to find answers within that will help you on the outside.

There are no quick fixes – we must embark on the voyage and as we find the courage to delve ever deeper into our personal wilderness, the greater are our rewards.

Of course, it would be easier to side-step our way through life without looking underneath the surface, although do we truly ever reach our potential or experience well-being if we shy away from self-understanding?

Given that it may have been some time since you read the first section, it is worth taking some time to recap on the general principles behind my *awaken your assertion* idea.   So, in this section, I'll summarise assertion's core elements and present them in a different way, in the spirit of engaging our proactive minds.

Assertive Principles and Values

There are three core principles behind authentic and consistent assertion and a handful of values, that when we honour, lead to improved results.

Principle 1 – The New Paradigm

In my experience, many assertiveness guides teach a *sticking plaster* approach and launch us only a little way down the path to success. To achieve genuine assertion, we must give attention to the new paradigm, which focuses on **introspection and self-awareness**.

Getting to the roots of *why we behave unassertively* is the magic to unlock. When we gain the all-important insights into the source of our behaviours, beliefs and thought patterns, we have all the resources we need to adjust our behaviour patterns – for good. With the courage to shine the light on ourselves, we can explore, appreciate, learn and change the way we think, feel and ultimately behave at a profound level. Without this depth of reflection, old habits reign supreme, leaving us to feel frustrated and dissatisfied with our inconsistent results.

When we look at ourselves, we access a whole heap of information that helps us fine-tune our behavioural engine to present, in the end, a far greater heart-centred existence. With a change to our spark plugs and some new oil, we can cruise through our work and personal lives with greater harmony and less conflict – surely this has to be on everyone's agenda?

Principle 2 – We Can Learn it!

Assertiveness is not something we are born with, it is a sophisticated art that we develop as we broaden our horizons and experiences. We **are** born with the primal reactions of *fight and flight,* which are innate, self-preservation behaviours, stimulated by a chemical defence mechanism inbuilt into our sub-conscious mind. When we acknowledge this, we arm ourselves with the opportunity to explore our unconscious patterns of behaviour, what has influenced their existence and their impact on our lives. This information then helps us to make informed decisions about how we need to change, given our goals and desires. It is only in the *unlearning* that we create the space to *relearn*.

Principle 3 – Hilltop of Experiences

The most dominant, primal instinct that drives our behaviour depends upon the environment within which we were raised and the people who had the most significant influence on our thoughts, beliefs and behaviours.

Our adult patterns emerge from the people and events that we were exposed to consistently during our childhood. Those patterns form the composition of our own personal *hilltop* upon which we view and interpret the world before us. As events, situations and people pass by we make judgements about how to handle them based on our hilltop's embedded reference points. If we have adopted a fear of upsetting people, then in the face of an argument we unconsciously find ourselves withdrawing, complying and following the path of least resistance, just to keep the peace.

The most influential people in our lives, positively or negatively shape our thoughts and beliefs, which lead to the creation of our habits. Our challenge is to tune into their teachings and review how constructive they are and what impact they are having on our effectiveness and well-being. Habits have a funny way of tripping us up and we find ourselves naturally blaming others for our mistakes.

Yet when we have the courage to look within, we find almost all the answers lying there, patiently waiting for our awakening. As we age and gain more experience, we eventually find alternative ways of achieving better results and more constructive, harmony-building techniques become the norm.

Yet to short-circuit this *eventual awakening*, we need to make a slight deviation along our unconscious path to the future. A reflective peek in the mirror will do the job. Investing time assessing how we operate, how our thinking patterns and external events trigger habitual behaviours, illuminates a fascinating and accelerated path to self-fulfilment and success.

Assertive Values – Philosophy Foundation

A number of core values collaborate with these three principles, providing support to our Assertive Philosophy, giving it definition and robustness. These values are best summarised in the grid:

I take responsibility for my thoughts, feelings and actions.	I am active and proactive in my behaviours and attitudes.	Integrity and the desire to be constructive drive me.
I respect other people's opinions even if they differ to mine.	I trust in myself.	I only change those things that are within my direct control.
Behaviours have consequences and I consider these before I act.	Fairness and equity sit at the heart of my interactions.	I am able to look within before judging others.
I value and appreciate people's differences.	I express myself in a direct, respectful and honest manner.	I assert my rights without violating the rights of others.
	Assertiveness starts and ends with me.	

By recognising the importance of the three principles and honouring these values, we can take the first few essential steps towards *authentic assertion*.

Assertive Values Exercise

 Using the values above, which do you honour easily and that thereby support your assertion? Which values feel less comfortable for you? These may indicate where you need to put your attention as you learn to become more assertive.

This can be such a useful exercise in understanding the fundamental blocks you have to specific situations, which we will discuss later.

Behavioural Characteristics

Investing in self-development work means we need to be prepared to assess our current effectiveness, styles and predominant behaviour patterns. It is only from here that we can move forward constructively.

In the first section, I presented a Behavioural Analysis Questionnaire and an accompanying Profile Summary, which provides a high-level assessment of our current patterns. Using the different behaviour patterns, we can begin to play around with the idea that these potential stereotypes can be dangerous at worst and limiting at best. We must acknowledge the interplay between each other so we can learn how to navigate through and adopt different styles when the situation requires.

Behavioural Spectrum – Marginal Differences

One way we can move beyond the dangers of stereotyping is to look at behaviours using the idea of a spectrum. Imagine a line with **zero** at the left-hand side - representing **Passive Behaviour. Ten** is at the right-hand side - representing **Aggressive Behaviour.** Sitting in the middle, **dissecting this spectrum is five** - representing **Assertive Behaviour.**

Each number, from *zero to ten*, indicates a level of intensity relevant to the broad characteristics of the behaviour categories. For example, **zero** represents extreme passivity, a 'wall flower', someone who is shy, is uncomfortable interacting and has little or no self-belief. Whilst **three** is still passive, this number demonstrates more confidence in interactions, although still shows signs of timidity and uncertainty.

At the other end of the spectrum, **ten** is the extreme picture of aggression, which would be violence, abuse and bullying. Yet **eight** might highlight a more sarcastic, arrogant and subtle aggression that has less intensity than its number ten counterpart.

Five is the ideal balance - the perfect assertion. Both **four and six** are both within its foothills, showing a slightly milder and strong presentation of assertion, sitting either side. This is what I call the *marginal difference*.

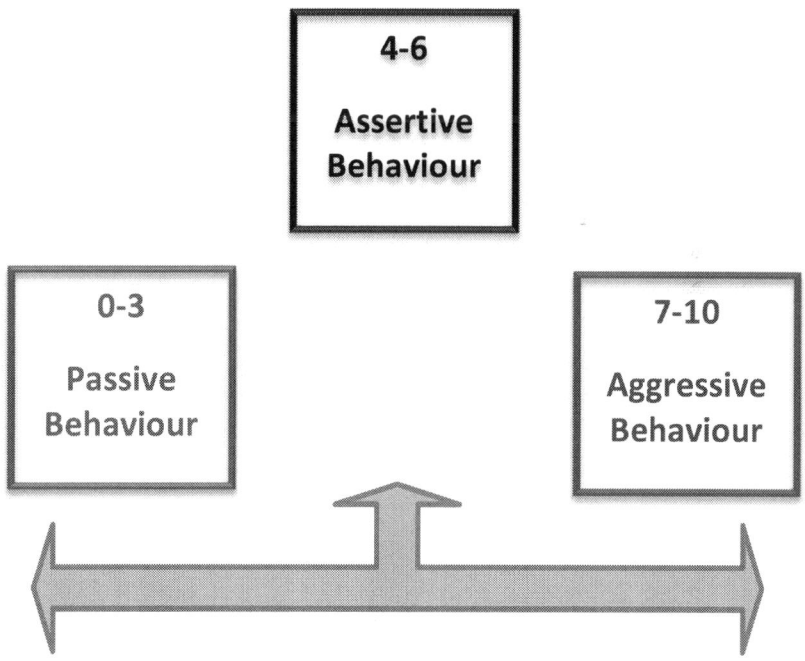

This model can be helpful in exploring:

- Where we predominantly operate
- Where we move to when we face a stressful situation.

A point worth mentioning here is that we are unlikely to remain just at one number for life. Various people and situations may provoke different reactions in us and these are worth examining. For example, we may operate predominantly at **three**, although there may be a family member whose energy zapping behaviour triggers frustration, prompting a leap-frog to **seven** in our interactions with them.

Often, if we sit predominantly at the lower end of the spectrum, we find it difficult to express our feelings and sometimes another person may behave in a way that tips us over the edge. Much like a champagne bottle, we explode and bubble over. We are then likely to experience remorse, guilt and regret for behaving 'out of character' and we very quickly return to our starting position three, until the next outburst.

Of course, the healthy alternative is to learn a more assertive approach, building the confidence to express ourselves more openly - so the leap-frogging behaviours are minimised, we protect our health and we restore our energy balance.

To bring this spectrum to life a bit more, let me use the playing card imagery; an exercise I often use during my Assertive Development workshops.

Imagine the scene. A group of ten people sitting in a room; each chooses a playing card at random, from Ace to 10. (There is no zero in a pack of cards, so we need to be a little adaptive). The cards are face down, so no one else knows the value of their card.

The group members must then contribute to a debate, adopting the behavioural characteristics that are most relevant to their card's number, using the spectrum idea from earlier. The group then identifies who has which card, indicated by their behavioural representation, which provokes an interesting conversation.

Focusing on the diverse behaviours that people display can be helpful in, not only understanding our own patterns, also understanding how to best interact with t hem to create a positive and constructive outcome.

Playing Card Exercise

If you had to identify **playing card 2**, what characteristics would you look for? What would they be saying, how would they be saying it and what body language would you see?

What if you had to pin-point **number 7**? What would their characteristics be?

If you had to define the *margins of difference* either side of **card 2** (i.e. 1 and 3) and **card 7**, (5 and 6), how would you tell them apart? What subtleties separate them?

Six Types of Assertion

Using this principle of marginal difference, we can now begin to explore the *assertive element* more fully, clarifying the behavioural subtleties involved.

The table below illustrates the *six types of assertion* we can access during an interaction. Referring to the spectrum from earlier, the points summarised below start around four/five, slowly rising, in small degrees, to seven. Please note that seven is not a conveyance of aggression, it is just a subtle increase in strength and must be appropriate to the situation and individual concerned.

Description	How to Use it	Communication Strategy
Basic Assertion 4-5	This is a statement of position, where we make our needs and feelings clear. Use it to give information, feedback to others or when raising an issue.	• "I need to be away by…" • "I feel pleased with…." • "The cost will be…" • "I haven't thought about that before, I need some time to reflect."
Empathic Assertion 5	This is a recognition of other's needs/feelings as well as our own. It is good for situations where there is a conflict as it avoids over-reacting with aggression by slowing down our response.	• I appreciate that, although…" • I know you're busy, although I really need this job done tonight." • I realise it is difficult to be precise, although a rough estimate will do."
Discrepancy Assertion 5-6	This strategy points out when there has been a discrepancy between an original agreement and the current reality. It is useful for clarifying misunderstandings or incongruent behaviour.	• "As I understand it, we agreed that… You have taken this action, so I'd like to clarify the priority." • "On the one hand…, on the other…. We need to agree the best way forward." • "There seems to be a discrepancy, what are our options?"

Negative Feelings Assertion **6**	This highlights the effect someone's behaviour is having and helps us deal with negative emotions more constructively, without outbursts and tantrums.	• "When you do this... it has this effect on me." **(objective statement of behaviour)** • I feel annoyed when this happens, so in future..." **(description of its effect)** • I'd prefer it if…" **(preference statement)**
Broken Record Assertion **4-6**	This is a progression of assertive styles, starting with the minimum affect to achieve our objective. Our assertion then strengthens, as the situation requires. The key is the message is unaltered, so it sounds consistent and robust, yet reinforces the intention.	**Basic** "We need to speed up our productivity to get the job done on time." **Empathic** "I understand that it means overtime for you, although it is critical we finish on time." **Consequences** "Productivity must improve or we will not be paid."
Consequence Assertion **6** **(may be 7 if absolutely necessary)**	This is a *last resort* response where it informs another of the consequences of their behaviour. Only use when there is authority and confidence to apply the sanctions.	• "If this continues, I'm left with no alternative." • I will not invest more time until you co-operate." • Being late is unacceptable. You must start on time or I must take formal action."

We may notice here, particularly in the last point, how slight the marginal difference between assertion and aggression is and this is why it is the 'last resort' alternative.

As with all these strategies, the key to keeping it in the assertive sector is **how** we deliver these phrases. The tone of our voice, volume, pitch, pace and body language that accompany these phrases will generate one behaviour or the other. Choose wisely!

By now we can start to see how assertiveness is not one panacea – it is a range, a fine-tuning, a basket of options that help us remain emotionally detached yet compassionate, calm, constructive and collaborative to create the right outcome that honours all parties.

Influencing Model

Assertiveness is about how we influence others to achieve common ground, compromise and a desired outcome. It is not about forcing, dragging, instructing, telling or demanding action. It is so much more subtle than this.

The model below focuses on how to gently pull people with us, guide or push them, using just a handful of natural interaction skills. The left-hand side of the model shows how, through practise of self-expression, we can motivate a movement in someone without force.

The right-hand side shows the sensitivity that *people-centred techniques* can achieve to magnetise movement towards a desired destination.

Please notice the softness in the words I have used to demonstrate the *assertive marginal difference* compared to the drag and shove that might be more akin to the aggressive camp.

Win-Win Model

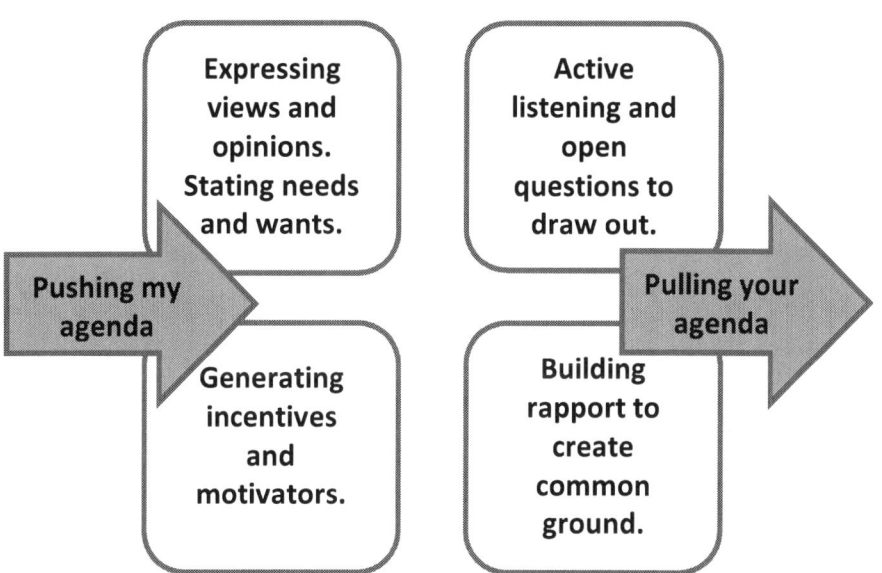

It is important to acknowledge here, that it is acceptable to push people and for it to be assertive; we just need to be mindful about *how* we do this. When there is force or ego behind it, then there is a danger that we move into an aggressive position.

The approach above is more about how we influence people to come with us rather than forcing action.

"What lies behind us and what lies beyond us are tiny matters compared to what lies within us."

Ralph Waldo Emerson

Chapter 3
Situational Assertion

"Different strokes for different folks."

Song Lyrics

Over the last twenty years of running Assertive Development workshops, I have had the pleasure of working with a diverse group of people who were looking to develop their skills for personal and professional reasons. Throughout these two decades, they have presented a range of scenarios that have evolved my workshops and my own understanding of this fascinating topic. It is, therefore, with gratitude to them all, that I sit here today writing this book.

Their problems challenged me in such a way that it enabled me to continue revising, colouring and re-evaluating the ever-changing needs of the business world, offering assertive solutions that they could personalise to match their own emerging authentic assertion.

One of the biggest lessons I learnt about my own assertion, was that situations and people are unique and so each one requires a different approach, set of tools and skills to achieve the best outcome. There is no *catch all* technique.

In addition, I realised that because of the formation of my own personal hilltop, there are some situations I feel more comfortable in than others. This has helped me keep focused on where I needed to develop *my* skills and confidence.

Your Situational Assertion

 Reflect on the situations that you feel most comfortable and confident in and the people in your network who bring out the best in you. Notice and write down what it is about them that triggers this more assertive response. Why are you confident in these situations?

Review those circumstances and people where you fall into the *avoidance trap*, feel awkward, passive, aggressive or just generally uncomfortable.

Examine what it is about those scenarios that do not bring out the best in you. What patterns and triggers do they provoke and what inner fears and anxieties arise when you think about them?

Using this information, now refer to the sections in this chapter that are best placed to help you develop your situational assertion.

The following pages are a collection of 'How to deal with…' scenarios that I hope help with the mastering of our day-to-day assertive challenges.

How to Negotiate and Compromise

So many participants over the years have longed to know how to get better results through negotiation. Although what amazed me was people's perception of what a negotiation sounded like. Cited examples often conveyed outright bully tactics that in today's environment are just not acceptable practice at all.

I guess it is fair to say that negotiation never really stops whether it's at work, in a shop, buying a new car or booking a hotel. We can base our success on **how** we deliver the negotiation message and the intent that drives our interaction in the first place. Here is my perspective on achieving great results using assertive negotiation skills.

Firstly, let us be clear what a negotiation is. The Collins English Dictionary describes *to negotiate* as:

Discuss with a view to a mutual settlement.

The two key words in this definition are ***discuss*** and ***mutual***. This is where most people fall down in their perception of what a negotiation is and why, I suspect, many of their attempts have failed.

Negotiation derives from a desire to improve upon a set of terms presented for our benefit or the advantage of a group. It is not a battle to win at all costs to feel victorious. This premise would place the other party in a lesser position than ourselves, which is of course not the principle behind assertive behaviour. The objective is to ensure that each party achieves a satisfactory *mutual settlement*.

Brian Tracy, motivational speaker and author, believes that

'Everything is negotiable'.

His thinking is that because all prices and terms are based on a *best guess* of what another is prepared to accept, there is always a potential movement, as those prices are rarely set in stone.

The art of negotiating a better deal, price or set of conditions, bases itself on the **quality of the discussion** we have and **the needs of the other party**. The gap between the two people negotiating is based on the true valuation of the settlement that meets both parties' needs. Therefore, the only issue we have is the different positions we both hold and how willing we are to manoeuvre towards each other's strong-hold.

The starting point to an assertive negotiation is having a positive intent behind the discussion, and not a mind-set that means to cheat or 'win over' the other party for our benefit. Instead, its intention is to achieve a movement in a given condition, such that an improved and beneficial settlement can be achieved.

Thirteen Top Tips for Assertive Negotiation

- **Know yourself.** Before entering a negotiation, we must understand our anxieties. As we have seen in the previous two sections, our fears, conditions and patterns drive us to succeed or trip us up. Look within and get to know our areas of discomfort. If typically we find negotiation an awkward situation, then identify what fears, past influences and patterns are blocking us. Once we have established those blocks and eliminated the irrational beliefs behind them, the skills I have listed below will help make negotiating an effortless art.

- **Be prepared before entering a negotiation.** Preparation is key to so many life skills, and negotiating is no different. We must give ourselves time to learn about the other parties involved and their possible perspectives. Think about what will be in it for them to reach a mutual agreement. Understand their position when they initially composed the conditions and what is driving their request. This helps us focus on any potential objections they may have when we enter the discussion and help them feel that they are getting something from the settlement.

- In addition, take time to think about what our desired outcome is for the negotiation. Consider carefully what the compromise is, where and how far we are willing to move and adjust our position accordingly. **Remember that the mutual agreement hides in the gap between *us* and the *other party*** and understanding both sides of the argument helps to uncover what is acceptable.

- **Know the audience.** Establish the position of the other person in the discussion. The *best guess* will have been shaped around a set of parameters that needs to be met and understanding their stand-point is an important phase of the negotiation. They may not have set the conditions in the first place, although are expected to assert them, such as in a shop.

- **Be willing to engage in a discussion**. If a condition or request seems unfair or impractical, then knowing we have an opportunity to negotiate the terms is step one. That requires a willingness to ask good quality, open questions that engages the other person in the discussion. Do not be distracted by the **fear of rejection or disapproval** as it is in our or another's interest, to negotiate a better set of terms.

- **Be courageous in our requests** for a price or condition. Start high and we can always come down. *Courage* and *elimination of fears* are central to a good quality negotiation.

- **Combine the negotiating request with confidence, calmness and expectation**. If we enter a discussion, believing we will not achieve our desired outcome, then we are more likely to fail. Believe that what we want will come to us.

- **Enter the negotiation with a statement of intent and a question** that uses positive language and an invitation to engage. Phrases such as:

  - *"I need to talk to you about X, when would be a good time?"*
  - *"I need to talk about X, who is the best person to talk to?"*
  - *"I am quite surprised by what you've asked for here and need to discuss what scope there is for flexing around it."*
  - *"You have asked for X, which I need to discuss with you. What is behind your request?"*
  - *"I am having difficulties delivering this, what's your final deadline?"*
  - *"I understand that you need X doing by Y and my team is not free until A. What help can you give us in expanding the deadline so we can do a high quality job for you?"*

- **Negotiation is always two-way.** Make sure that we build the ***What's In It For Me*** (WIIFM). The other party needs to experience a 'win' as well as us achieving our goal, so ensure that we offer a benefit to any possible manoeuvre.

- **Remain calm at all times, focusing on facts not emotion.** Amateur negotiators get emotionally involved in the discussion when not getting their way, becoming demanding, angry or rude. This is not a negotiation; this is a one-way argument. This type of approach puts the other person's back up and whilst it may temporarily get the result, it does nothing for the on-going relationship and any future negotiations that may be required. Keep cool, even if the other person is emotional, using phrases such as:

  - *"I understand (or appreciate) what you are saying, although I feel strongly that..."*
  - *"I need to find a way to..."*
  - *"I acknowledge that this is difficult, although we need to find some middle ground."*
  - *Use the Broken Record technique, repeating the same positive phrases, just in a different order or with a different emphasis.*

- **Change tact if there is resistance.** If the negotiation comes up against an aggressor who is unwilling to manoeuvre, then consider the best course of action. We may decide that no result is better than a confrontation or we may feel that it is appropriate to talk to another party. Consider the situation, the importance of the result and the relationship with the individual before deciding how far we need to take the discussion.

- **Ensure the negotiation is with the right person.** There is no point entering a discussion if it is with someone who does not have the power, position or ability to agree to the new terms. Always make sure that we are talking to the decision maker.

- **50% of something is better than 100% of nothing.** Know when the limit of the settlement has been reached. If we push for more, we may destroy any good-will we have built up. Remember that negotiation is not about winning at all odds, it is about improving the terms of condition, price or request. We will need to make a judgement about the principle of the negotiation *versus* the amount of time we are investing in the settlement, because our time is a valuable asset.

- **Appreciate the settlement we have reached.** Honour the relationship in readiness for any future interactions by appreciating them, their willingness to negotiate and the result achieved. It is not about thanking them profusely in a people-pleasing manner, although it is about valuing our interaction and the compromise reached.

How to Say 'No', Without Feeling Guilty

When I think back to the Assertiveness courses I have run, without fail, each workshop had at least one participant asking for improved capability in saying 'no'. It was as certain at turning on the tap and getting a flow of water. Here are my thoughts on this very popular topic, honouring the possibility that this may be an important topic for you too. **Why is saying 'No' difficult?**

Understanding Saying 'No' Challenges

The first thing I would like you to consider is why 'no' seems like such a difficult word to say.

- What emotions does it bring up for you?
- What fear is at the root of your discomfort?
- What do you worry about losing if you were to say 'no'?
- What price do you pay for your repeated compliance?

When you understand the answer to these questions, then you can focus your effort on resolving these issues by referring to the first two sections, which will help you tremendously.

Understanding Our 'No's

- If our predominant pattern is passive, then saying 'no' is tricky. We may say it confidently in our head, although saying it aloud is virtually impossible for fear of upsetting another. This means we develop a pattern of compliance, which honours the other person and not ourselves. This approach leaves behind it a trail of internal conflict, because we know we should say 'no', although we are driven almost completely by fear of losing something.

- It is worth understanding the irrational beliefs around our saying 'no' issues to help us unravel the intricate web of discomfort. Here are just some strands that weave their thread:

  - Saying 'no' is aggressive and rude and people may therefore dislike me.

  - It might show me up as being difficult, awkward or stubborn.

  - It might irritate them and this may affect our friendship or my performance review.

  - Being compliant is important, as I was taught as a child to 'do as I was told.'

  - Other people's needs are more important than mine are.

  - If I have been asked to do something by someone in authority, I must do as I am told.

  - Saying 'no' might sound petty and selfish.

  - Other people may feel rejected if I turn them down or say 'no'.

- As we found out in the second part of the book, we learn our beliefs and conditioning, primarily through our childhood experiences and influences. Once we have identified our irrational beliefs, we are then free to re-programme our mind with healthier, more assertive beliefs through working our mental muscle. To help us along the way, here are some constructive beliefs to consider:

- I have the right to voice my opinion even if it differs to others.

- Differing opinions simply create discussion.

- In honouring myself first, others get a better result from me in the end.

- A 'no' is not a rejection.

- Saying 'no' is not about refusing the person; it is about refusing the situation.

- If aggression is a more dominant pattern for us, then 'no' is a common word in our internal dictionary and we have very little hesitation in using it. It is most likely to have a very specific tone to it and it is often accompanied with a hint of sarcasm:

  - 'Err, no.'

  - 'No way.'

  - 'You have to be joking – no.'

  - 'No, not a chance.'

  - 'Not in this lifetime.'

  - 'Dream on.'

Strategies for Making 'No' Easier

From an assertiveness view-point, I prefer to move away from the notion of simply saying 'no', which reduces the discomfort and removes the emotional attachment that accompanies it. Consider this response to a work request for our time by someone from another team member:

'I'm busy right now, although I will be free in about half-an-hour, when I'd be happy to help you. How does that sound?'

This phrase does four things:

- It makes a clear statement that honours us.
- It demonstrates clear boundaries.
- It shows a willingness to help.
- It engages the other party in a discussion through the open question.

If we take this scenario forward and assume that the requestor does not like the sound of our proposal, here is how we might tackle their retort:

'No that's unacceptable, I need it done now.'

'I'm sorry that we can't make that work. As I said, I will be free and happy to help in 30 minutes. Perhaps you could speak to one of my colleagues and ask for their help on this occasion.'

Now if the requestor happens to be the boss, we could say;

'When does this task need to be done by, as I have something that needs completing, which will take me thirty minutes?

If it needs to be done now, then can you either pass on this task to someone else or could you take it off me to free me up?'

What this approach does is show that we are standing up for our position and honouring it, remaining firm and offering alternatives, without being difficult, awkward or aggressive. 90% of the time, the first response produces a positive outcome, although if we are presented with obstruction and stubbornness, then we use the ***Broken Record Technique*** to hold a firm position.

Six Ways to Say 'No'

In addition to these real-life examples, here are a further six techniques for refusing a request without feeling guilty. They come from UK psychologist Trevor Powell.

- **The Direct 'no'** - If we are asked to do something we can't or do not want to, just say 'no'. Yet this may feel difficult depending upon our irrational beliefs. The aim is saying 'no' without feeling that we must apologise, although as we start out on this saying 'no' journey, it may feel less aggressive to say, *'I'm sorry, I can't do that.'* *'I can't attend, I'm sorry.'* Over time, I suggest that we practise without the apology, as it is not always necessary.

- **The reflecting 'no'** - This involves acknowledging the content and sentiments of the request, then adding our assertive refusal at the end. For example, *'I know I need to deliver that today, although tomorrow is looking more likely.'* This technique shows an emotionally intelligent quality to our interaction.

- **The reasoned 'no'**. Give a very brief and genuine reason why we are saying 'no'; *'I can't have lunch with you because I have a job that needs to be finished by tomorrow.'*

- **The rain-check 'no'**. This is my favourite type of 'no' because inadvertently it is a 'yes'. Psychologically the person requesting still gets what they need, although in a different timescale. It is a way of saying 'no' to the request at the present moment and gives us scope for saying 'yes' in the future. For example, *'I can't have lunch with you today, although I could make it sometime next week.'*

- **The enquiring 'no'**. As with the rain-check 'no', this is not a definite 'no'. It is a way of opening up the request to see if there is an alternative. For example, *'I am involved in doing an important job this afternoon. Is there anyone else who could help you?'*

- **The broken record 'no'**. We can use this in a wide range of situations. We just repeat the simple statement of refusal. No explanation, just repeat it. It is particularly good for persistent requests. *'I can't do it right now; I can definitely do it tomorrow.'* *'As I said, I can't do it now.* We notice how the broken record technique increases up the spectrum scale that we discussed earlier. We must be mindful of the tone of voice and body language we use to accompany this phrase, as it would be easy for this to scale up from a five to an eight if we became frustrated.

How to Handle Conflict

For those of us who demonstrate a pattern of people-pleasing passivity, handling conflict is a big concern and often we play out a fantastic episode of avoidance and compliance. The consequence of this behaviour is that we constantly put our needs secondary to others, lacking the confidence to express our opinions and, at its extreme, people walk all over us.

It is important to acknowledge the two-stage approach with conflict. Firstly, there is *prevention*, which ensures conflict does not arise in the first place. Secondly, we have *survival* if we find ourselves in the conflict already, then there are some tips about what to do when we are in the vortex.

Before we discuss these approaches, here is a definition to get us started:

Conflict occurs when two or more values, perspectives or opinions are contradictory in nature and are not aligned, agreed or discussed.

Prevention - Understanding what Causes Conflict

When we recognise the source of a conflict, we are better able to resolve it and even prevent it from happening. By understanding what activates a potential conflict and being aware of the trigger points, we can behave in a more proactive and mindful manner, preventing a confrontation from arising. Here is a summary of some of the main causes:

Group diversity - when a group comes together, they bring:
- Different values, attitudes and beliefs
- Different views of the world – hilltops
- Individual styles and approaches.

Poor communication can lead to conflicts when there is a:
- Miscommunication in what is said or heard
- Incongruence in message to body language

- No communication is offered at all so people are left to make up their own stories
- Lack of understanding when a message conveyed – no checks are made to ensure that the message given is the message understood
- 'Grapevine' is trusted, which creates a 'blown up' issue
- Lack of clarity over what is expected.

Ineffective leadership, when at work, in particular where there is:

- Inconsistent leadership
- Little or no follow-through on decisions
- No involvement
- No compassion or integrity.

When we feel threatened, we react emotionally, triggered by:

- Unwanted or poor feedback/criticism
- When feeling attacked by another
- When our basic needs are attacked.

Internal turmoil causes a majority of conflict issues, arising from:

- Values and attitudes not being aligned
- Fears at the potential loss of something
- Anxieties created by a difference between our 'ideal' v 'reality'.

Techniques for Dealing with Conflict

Coping with Arising Conflict	Resolving Conflict Confidently
Stop, Think, Choose.	Appreciate other's situation – use the Hilltops model.
Notice our reaction and internal dialogue.	Take the initiative, be in control and choose an appropriate response.
Assess what values, opinions or attitudes are out of line.	Listen and ask open questions that creates understanding.
Respond not react – buy time to think before we act.	Empathise sensitively and not patronisingly.
Consider the most appropriate option, considering their position.	Be open and honest about how we feel.
See things through another's eyes and see how things might look.	Use appreciations such as, I agree, I understand, I appreciate.
Remember their hilltops – we are all different.	Use powerful language such as; I feel, I believe, I noticed.
If the conflict is a reaction to someone's behaviour, remember their behaviour is expressing a NEED to be met.	When giving feedback, remember to depersonalise and focus on the behaviour/action and not the personality of the individual.
We have a right to our opinions.	Assert our right to self-expression.
FEAR is False Expectations Appearing Real. Keep rational.	Keep good eye contact with the individual, asserting our position.

Consider what our desired outcome is and head for a win/win.	Use the broken record technique if we are not heard.
Believe in ourselves and recall the impact SID has on our actions.	Plan what we want to say and how we are going to say it.
Remain rational and maintain a positive perspective.	Take responsibility and accept our role in the conflict.
Realise that conflict can create a positive interaction and therefore is not something to be feared.	Engage others in a conversation rather than arguing and explore why they feel as they do.
Choose not to engage.	It is ok to agree to disagree.

Specific Assertive Behaviours to Resolve Conflict

- **Use 'I' statements.** Let the other party know how we **feel** when the conflict is occurring. Let them know which of our rights we feel is being ignored.

- **Speak calmly, coolly and rationally,** so that they listen to and respect us more. Otherwise, they may go on the defensive.

- **Avoid blaming.** This will keep the communication flow going. It encourages understanding and empathy for each other's feelings. It recognises that for most conflict to exist there must be at least two parties involved.

- **Be willing to forgive.** Forgiveness is a powerful tool. We have a chance for personal growth by forgiving others for their part in the hurt and pain we have suffered. At times, this is the only way to resolve a conflict.

- **Be willing to forget.** Once we have resolved a conflict, let go of the issue. Once we have implemented an agreed resolution, get it out of our minds.

- **Be honest.** It is imperative that we are honest with ourselves and others about our feelings and reactions to the conflict. If we behave compliantly and untruthfully, then the conflict's resolution is a false one and the conflict will recur. We gain nothing by being dishonest in the management of conflict. We waste our time and energy and end up feeling a failure or guilty.

- **Focus on feelings rather than on the content.** Effective listening is key in the productive resolution of conflict. Listen for their emotions and reflect empathy and understanding. This creates an atmosphere of compassion and reduces defensiveness. It focuses on the process involved rather than on the issues and it brings the parties to a clearer recognition of their individuality and humanity.

- **Show respect for ourselves and for others.** We gain more in resolving a conflict through respect than by disrespect e.g. being vindictive, taking revenge, threatening, yelling, accusing, belittling, ostracising, ignoring. If we are on the receiving end of disrespect, remove ourselves as soon as possible and continue the discussion when everyone has 'cooled down'. If we become disrespectful, stop as soon as possible by either removing or silencing ourselves.

- **Be willing to apologise or admit a mistake.** It is necessary to admit to a mistake and to apologise for our behaviour before a stalemate can be achieved. It takes courage, character, and fortitude to admit an error.

- **Be willing to compromise.** If we cling to our opinion as the 'right and only one' we close out the other person's view. To succeed in resolving conflict, all parties must feel like they have gained in the resolution. Only through compromise can we both feel like a winner.

How to Handle Aggression

Let's face it, however assertive we are, we will always come across aggressors. Equipping ourselves with the right tools to remain calm and handle the situation constructively is key.

We are likely to experience two different types of aggression:

1. Someone else's aggression

2. Our own internal aggression, triggered by anger, frustration or irritation.

Someone else's Aggression

As we have explored, our behaviour has its roots in our beliefs, conditioning, values and past influences. When faced with a situation, we make decisions about how to behave by unconsciously consulting our deeply engrained reference points, held within our subconscious mind. Based on those pointers, we unconsciously feel an emotion, think a thought and ultimately adopt a behaviour that we display, creating an interaction.

Behind the two primal behaviours of aggression and passivity is an unconscious need to feel safe, secure, loved, accepted and worthy. For example, a compliant behaviour is a subliminal message of *'Please like and approve of me.'* An aggressive, dominant behaviour can be a message that says, *'I need to dominate you so that I feel better about myself.'*

Added to this is that our behaviour is dominated instinctively by a set of core values that form the basis of how we interpret our world and how we interact with another person.

For example, say we have a strong value around *respecting others* and *courtesy*. If we are faced with a shop assistant who is rude or perhaps disengaged with us, we could find ourselves feeling frustrated or annoyed, triggered by their behaviour towards us. As a result, we start reacting aggressively towards them and raise the potential for a confrontation.

151

The key to this scenario is to remember that it is not that individual who has *made us mad*, it is our internal reaction to their behaviour, which our programming triggers. They are behaving a certain way because of their internal programming and not because of us.

When we understand this, it disassociates us from the aggression and allows us to interact more constructively and compassionately. We start to consider the other person has their own 'stuff' that influences their behaviour and this understanding can prevent us from reacting. Sometimes just the simplicity of a smile can interrupt their aggressive pattern – try it – it works!

With this basic premise in place, here is one fabulous technique for dealing with aggressors:

Fogging Technique

Fogging helps us to *respond* to the situation and not instinctively *react*. This strategy slows aggressors down by an unexpected response. It helps us to remain calm, side-step their issue and yet still retaining our point of view and integrity by agreeing with only some part of what they say.

It robs the aggressor of their destructive power and whilst superficially it may seem like a submissive response, it is in fact assertive because of its implication. By refusing to become upset or angry, we are able to remain detached from the situation, which temporarily dis-empowers them.

We call it fogging because the effect is like suddenly facing a blanket of fog when the way appeared to be clear. Imagine what we would do if we were driving along in clear weather and then faced a bank of fog.

It unsettles us for a time and makes us refocus. Here is an example.

'I can't believe that the company are treating me like this – what have I ever done to deserve this treatment?'

'Yes, I can understand that you must feel shocked by this treatment. Let's talk about what the options are for resolving this.'

The word **YES**, takes an aggressor by surprise and puts the brakes on. The objective of fogging is to give us time to get our assertive response together – not to be evasive. Here are some other ways to fog the aggressor:

- **Agree with the truth** – find a component in their conversation that is truthful, and agree with that statement.

- **Agree with the odds** – agree with any possible truth in the statement.

- **Agree in principle** – agree with the general truth in a logical statement such as, 'That makes sense.'

Other phrases typically used when fogging are:

- That could be true

- You are probably right

- Sometimes I think so myself

- I agree, I understand, I appreciate

- That is true

- You are right

- You have a point there

Our Own Internal Aggression

During the course of this Assertive Development Journey, we have talked about what influences our thoughts, feelings and behaviours. We should be well on our way to shifting the predominant patterns that have shown up in our lives and delivered, up until now, less than constructive results.

Although in reality, anger may still arise because there are going to be some primal instincts, which some people and situations will trigger within us. It is chemical and it is what makes us human. Being assertive does not mean that we enter a dream-like cartoon, where everything is rosy - the world is just not like that and nor are we.

Here are some additional techniques and thoughts that may help to curb a rising negative emotion:

- **Accept anger as a powerful resource** – a fuel, if we choose to use it from an assertive stand-point. Author and Coach, Christian Pankhurst has a fascinating opinion about how anger is necessary for our well-being, happiness and success. He describes anger as an elemental, primal source of energy that we simply need to refine.

- With our newfound self-awareness, when we accept anger as a primal emotion, we can use its energy as a natural fire, a passion that with the right communication channels can be expressed healthily to others. Recognise that the *sharp, angular anger* comes from a place of the unconscious; *refined anger* communicated with strength, assertion and self-worth, comes from place of self-awareness and acceptance of its fuel.

- **Channel negative emotion into a constructive interaction.** When we have moved beyond the 'anger is bad' view-point, we can explore how to use communication more effectively to convey our emotions. Again, when we stand in an assertive space, we think rationally about how we feel, what has triggered the anger and then talk to others about those feelings. Use the *Traffic Light, Stop, Think and Choose* strategy I mentioned earlier to refine anger into fuel. Then use language like, 'I feel angry about this.' 'That conversation hurt me because...' 'I am really disappointed by what has happened.'

- **Anger is a natural assertion when conveyed with awareness.** Remember that anger, which fuels our aggression, is an emotion; we cannot and must not stop it. When asserted, it demonstrates a degree of self-worth and boundaries that say, 'This is not acceptable to me and I need to express this.' The key is how we present our anger and do it with awareness.

- **Accept that it is ok for other people to think and feel differently to us.** When we operate from this space, then we find ourselves getting less angry and irritated. When we see the world from someone else's *hilltop* and learn to appreciate our differences – compassion and understanding dampens the sharpness of our anger and channels it more constructively.

- **Remove ourselves from the situation to contain the fire.** If the chemical reaction and our mouths have combined too quickly in the venting of our emotion, then quickly notice what is going on and choose to step away from the situation. When we remove ourselves from the situation that is trigger, then we can control the fire and channel it more healthily.

- **Notice our emotional triggers.** Our expectations, standards and values create the source for our negative emotions. When we are perfectionist and principled, people will consistently fail to meet our model of the world and we end up living in constant disappointment. When we understand our triggers and accept that other people are just different, not better or worse, this lessens the annoyance we feel about someone's behaviour, performance or standards.

- **Write down aggressive patterns.** When we notice a consistent trigger that 'makes our blood boil', it can be useful to write it down and map out what is going on behind our behaviour. When we explore what is happening and who is involved we can deal with the trigger proactively. Remember it is unlikely to be the individual or the situation per se, rather something that they represent for us that activates an emotional response. Once we have surfaced this we can then review if this pattern is constructive to hold onto and, if not, choose to change the pattern by using the techniques I outlined in section two, **Creating Unshakeable Self-Esteem**.

- **Rehearse what we want to say.** Thinking about what we want to say before we say it is always good practice, especially if we are feeling emotional and uptight. With a degree of discipline, when we learn to respond rather than react, using the principles I have outlined above, we can get to a place where we can begin to make sure 'our brain is in gear before opening mouth', as my gorgeous dad used to tell me as a child! Thinking about what outcome we want to achieve, how we might say it and what the consequences of that conversation could be, all help us find a more constructive space to start from.

- **Communication is the heart of positive relationships**. When we have the courage to accept that we have aggressive tendencies and we know what triggers our outbursts, then we are one step closer to getting in control. We can then forge constructive relationships by talking to people who trigger an aggressive reaction and discuss with them the impact their behaviour has on us. Setting boundaries and communicating these clearly to other people will prevent future outbursts from destroying or straining relationships, both at home and at work.

How to Build Rapport and Good Relationships

The art of relationship building is not always as easy as we think. *As a child*, it seems effortless and we bumble our way in and out of friendships without a second thought. *As adults*, for some reason it seems harder as we invest more into our connections and the price we pay for break ups increases.

Relationships form the basis of the web that connects us within businesses, across the globe and that sustain our communities. Without them, we are merely empty vessels of transactional matter.

When we talk about assertiveness, we need to give some space to the art that is *building relationships*. When we master that art, the effortlessness we experienced in our childhood can return to give our lives the well-being and harmony that are too often missing.

Building Empathy and Connection

We can define empathy as **the ability to understand and share the feelings of others**. This suggests that we need to employ a certain set of skills that enables understanding and sharing.

Very often, during the course of a formal interaction, our attention remains in a highly transactional plane, where we focus on the business at hand. This becomes a very outcome-driven conversation that does very little to foster a positive *understanding* and *sharing* with the other party. This may well be appropriate for some interactions. Although, consider for a moment how much more could be achieved by creating a greater connection with that individual or group.

The benefits of creating connections with people are:

- Less conflict
- Easier conflict resolution
- Joint problem solving
- Healthier discussions that encourage co-operation
- Greater opportunity and willingness to collaborate
- Sharing of resources and ideas
- Healthier negotiations
- Increased sales, improved service, greater quality
- Easier 'difficult conversations'
- Greater support.

The model below demonstrates the flow of a typical interaction, which can be applied to many of our interactions, where we end up being slightly dettached.

To really build and maintain relationships, we need to enter a conversation at an emotional level, building rapport and understanding. Then we can safely and smoothly move into the transactional plane where the majority of the interaction will take place in an assertive manner. And, if you exit at the emotional level, we leave the other person feeling supported and personally dealt with.

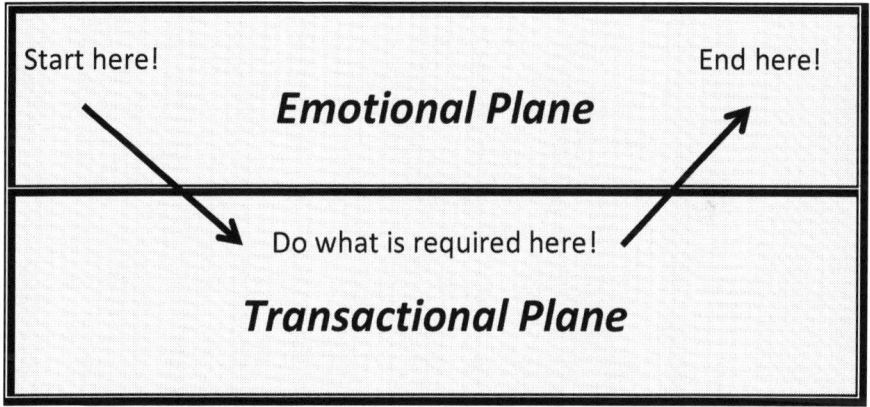

We can build empathy and connection in the following ways:

- Enter into a conversation with the **attitude of respecting differences and diversity**.

- Ask an **open question** that enquires about them, their health, family, business or holiday.

- If appropriate, **make notes** of what they say about themselves for future conversations.

- Be prepared to **disclose information about ourselves**, if asked by the other party or offer it up voluntarily in response to some common ground shared.

- Demonstrate that we **value them** by listening actively. People like and need to be heard.

- **Mirror and match their body language** (if face-to-face with them) so we can subliminally connect with them. Give them active eye contact to show attentiveness.

- Use the **same language**, tone and pace where possible during a conversation.

- If the relationship is one that we interact with on a daily basis, invest time in **getting to know the person**. Listen out for what motivates them, what their values and beliefs are and any self-esteem issues.

- **Offer support** and encouragement where appropriate.

- If on the phone, turn off and **remove all distractions** from our eye-line so that we can focus our attention totally on the other person.

- If our conversation is sensitive in nature, perhaps say in the work place, **find a private room** to talk so the other person is encouraged to open up.

- **Have sensitive conversations in person** and not via email or text.

Rebuilding a Broken Relationship

If there are relationships in our network that feel frayed, strained or broken and we have the desire to fix them, then look no further. The following steps provide a guide towards reconciliation.

When the Breakdown Occurs

- The breakdown may have caused some heat and emotion, so perhaps best to leave things to **cool down** for a while.

- **Understanding** is the next step to take. Take some time to think about what happened during the breakdown without over-analysing. Consider what contribution we had to it and what responsibility we need to accept.

159

- Think about how the other person might be feeling and **appreciate their perspective**.

- Think about how we will **approach them** to begin recovering the relationship.

- If we feel that an **apology is appropriate** and justified, then only do it if we are genuine.

- Consider how to **communicate** the recovery.

- Remember to change something about our relationship, think about **what we can change**, not about what we would like someone else to do differently.

Approaching the Recovery

- Suggest that it would be useful to **talk about what happened** between us and communicate our desire to solve the situation.

- **Meet somewhere neutral** where possible. Remember that we are initiating a recovery and feel good about this. Avoid re-igniting the discussion by going over old ground.

- Ask the person **what they believe was the cause of the problem** and listen actively to them.

- If anger or emotion arises again, avoid reacting to this. **Remain calm** and remember not to personalise it. State clearly what our feelings are about the situation.

- **State our view of the problem**, even if this is different to theirs.

- **Ask open questions** to clarify understanding and avoid reacting to what they are saying.

- Avoid making the discussions personal. **Keep objective** and stick to the important points. If they make personal comments, avoid taking them to heart. Listen to them and if necessary ask for clarification.

- Accept that a difference of opinion has occurred and, if necessary, **agree to disagree**. Outline what we can take responsibility for in the breakdown early in the discussion to encourage a non-hostile response.

- Enter into some **problem-solving discussions** with them and together decide how to best move forward.

- Be prepared to **negotiate and compromise** with them.

- **Build on the other person's ideas** and acknowledge them.

- **Acknowledge our achievements together** and exit the conversation on the emotional plane.

After the Recovery

- Find an early opportunity **to build rapport** with the person, using supportive language.

- **Use positive body language** and smile to reinforce our recovery.

- **Avoid replaying the events** leading up to the breakdown, in our minds. It is history now and our recovery should begin to build new foundations.

- Take time to **get to know the person** and disclose some things about ourselves that encourages trust building.

- If the other person continues to bring up past problems, then **talk about how it could be better** in the future, acknowledging rather than dismissing their opinions.

- **Communication is the key** throughout this process, so continue open and clear interactions.

Handling Difficult Situations

Now whilst I appreciate that this may be a more work-focused topic, I thought it was still useful to add this in, especially as we often find ourselves caught up in giving friends difficult messages or feedback. This one remains high on the list of stressful situations for most people and so this section promotes some very specific techniques that might help if this situation relates to you.

In my experience, anxieties around these types of difficult conversations can be broken down into the following concerns:

- What if they cry?

- What if they deny it and try to cover it up?

- What if they become aggressive towards me?

- What if they storm out?

- What if they don't like me any more?

- What if they gang up on me or make me pay?

- What if they whinge to others about me and undermine our friendship?

- What if they blame someone else and the problem just continues?

These are all very real reactions to our fear of these conversations and perhaps all eight of them appear in our fear repertoire. Anxieties like these prevent us from having the relationships we deserve.

Sometimes a friendship needs to have a driver, somone who is willing to take the 'bull by the horns' and tackle something that feels difficult or awkward. It's too easy to avoid these issues, procrastinate or ignore them, hoping that they will go away. Sadly they don't go away, often they simply get worse unless we find the courage to deal with it and be the driver.

What type of issues might we be looking at? Here is a sample of issues that have come up from past participants:

- Someone who has strong or unpleasant body odour

- A friend or family member who constantly interrupts, undermines or dominates us

- Someone who makes plans without consulting us

- Someone who is rude to another, either obviously or indirectly

- Having to correct someone who is wrongly or inappropriately giving advice

- Giving feedback to a partner where their behaviour towards us has been hurtful, upsetting or undermining

- A resentment that has been building around a family member's lack of consideration or thought for others

- An unplanned incident that requires us to think on our feet and respond to someone who is aggressive or attacking towards us

- Work based performance, competence and behavioural issues.

Handling Difficult Situations

If this is a relevant challenge to you, then it would be worth exploring in more depth what troubles you about these situations.

Reflect on what has caused, or might cause you anxiety when you think about situations that you class as difficult, whether they are personal, social or professional. Be aware of what triggers you to feel that way and explore the root of your concerns.

Then, given the techniques we have discussed in the previous two books, what SID's (Self Imposed Doubts) and fears might you need to address that will help alleviate your anxieties?

Tackling Feedback Assertively

As with all of the challenges I have raised in this chapter, the resolution primarily starts with us. If we can identify what causes our discomfort and are willing to address this, then we are half way to achieving a better outcome.

When we realise that much of our dis-ease is sourced in a fear of being disliked, then we have the key to unlocking our potential.

On the surface, an aggressor may seem as though they do not care about anyone else's feelings. Although, as we now know, an aggressor is very often dogged by the same low self-esteem issues as those who are submissive. Superficially they may seem unaffected, although the internal stress and anxiety simply fuels further aggression in the pursuit of gaining control and not being seen as weak.

Here are some well-grounded strategies for handling difficult situations more confidently:

- *'Listen with your eyes and hear with your heart.'* This is a lovely quote that I've used on many an Assertiveness Workshop. It focuses on how we interact with people. When we make a decision to behave with compassion then we experience things differently. Observing how friends, family or colleagues operate and looking beyond the behavioural issue rather than judging them, creates an empathic approach that sets out a much calmer place from which to start a discussion.

- *Look for patterns of behaviours.* Sometimes we are very quick to pounce on an issue and whilst we need to be mindful of the timing, observing someone's patterns gives us more evidence to work with, rather than reacting to what might be a one-off incident.

- *Collect concrete evidence not hear-say.* People will respond more favourably when there are tangible examples of what they have been doing. Often I hear people reporting 'I have been told by X, that you have done Y.' This is such an unhelpful opening. We must share **our** experience of their behaviour and not be shaped by what another has observed.

- *Timing and planning are essential.* Fears and anxieties often influence us to put off a difficult discussion, although responding to something in a timely way is important, once we have seen a pattern of behaviour emerging. Obviously, if there is a completely inappropriate display of behaviour such as rudeness, swearing or an outburst, then responding immediately might be appropriate, especially in work situation. Before entering a discussion, it is important to think about what we want to say and what outcome we need to achieve.

- *Focus on the behaviour not the person.* People often react defensively when they feel attacked or threatened. So comments like, 'You were so aggressive.' 'You didn't handle that very well.' 'You can't treat someone like that', are all likely to get us an unconstructive reaction. The 'you' is the key to the threat and sounds very accusatory.

  Instead use phrases like, '**I noticed that** you **seemed** upset during that phonecall.' 'When I asked you to complete that task, **you seemed** uncomfortable.' '**Tell me about** that call you had, as by your reaction, I felt that it hadn't gone so well.'

  The difference in emphasis and language, means that our feedback is less attacking. The responsibililty is firmly with our observations about their behaviour and it opens up an invitation to engage, which results in a more constructive discussion.

- *Be clear about the issue.* Hopefully the above approach will keep the discussion constructive and give the person permission to open up. Although if they are blind to the issue, it is important to be very clear about our observations, expectations and what specifically is inappropriate. The person must go away certain about their behaviour and the impact that has on our relationship or other people around us.

- **Keep discussions private.** For work placed discussions, this may seem like common sense although I have seen many performance talks happen in the public arena, which is tantamount to disaster. A public debate does nothing for the protection of the individual's welfare. A private room is essential.

- **Open with an invitation to engage.** Again in the work place situation, if we want to achieve a positive outcome for our feedback discussion, then engaging the person in conversation is key to our success. If they feel involved then we have a better chance of moving forward. Use phrases such as, 'Tell me about,' 'How did you feel when,' 'What happened this morning,' 'What's going on for you right now?' Opening up the conversation in this way often allows them to report the very performance issue that we need to pick up with them, which enabling us to simply agree with what they are saying and explore how to deal with the issue together. This approach is less effective with conversations with friends or family as it sounds too transactional. Simply use 'Can we talk?'

- **Use open questions to explore.** To prevent the person becoming defensive, enter the conversation with the intention of exploring and helping. Use open questions (Who, Why, What, When, Where and How) to get the person to open up, explore reasons for their behaviour and find solutions to preventing it in the future. If they blame someone else, again, use open questions to explore their perspectives and be prepared to offer an alternative view.

- **Offer help.** Everyone deserves a chance to change and if we keep the discussion open, we can focus on helping to improve the situation. Ask what we can do to help them, ask what commitments they need support with and focus on coaching them through the challenges rather than dictating what needs to happen.

- **Get commitments.** At the end of the conversation we need to close the discussion positively and provide some encouragement and affirmation where we can. Whilst this is not appropriate for all discussions, more often than not it will help the person see that they are supported and valued. Secure commitments that they will make to change the situation and ensure they are equipped to honour those actions.

- *Make notes for work place performance discussions.* In any type of performance issue, it is important to take notes of the conversation, even if it is of an informal nature. This not about *marking someone's copy book,* although it does give everyone clarity about what was discussed and agreed. It also provides a record for follow up conversations to track progress or take to the next level if poor performance continues.

- *Be prepared to think on our feet.* In all the situations above, we have some degree of control and an opportunity to think about what we want to say. When we are confronted by someone who is angry or upset then we may have less opportunity to create an assertive response. If this is the case, remember to breathe, listen and ask questions.

  These are all really important 'buying time' skills, which prevent us getting caught in the *reactive trap.* I find the 'Tell me more about that', can work well so we can gather ourselves, slow our heart-beat down and give the other person a chance to really vent their emotion. Also the deflective technique of 'I can see you are really upset about this', acknowledges how they are feeling and gives us a chance to gather ourselves.

- *If things get messy, step away.* If the conversation takes a turn for the worse despite our best efforts, then suggest the conversation is carried over to another time, when both parties are calmer. There is little point interacting when the atmosphere is highly charged with emotion.

- *Reflect on how the conversation went and be prepared to learn from mistakes.* Assertiveness is all about compassion and humility. Be prepared after a difficult conversation to reflect on how it went and what we could do differently next time. Learn from the experience and continually look to enhance our techniques and approaches.

Formal Work-based Performance Discussions

It is important to make a quick mention before we leave this section about the more formal performance discussions that may be needed in the work place.

The above suggestions are very much driven by a more informal conversation, although the reality of today's business is that performance issues centering on behaviours, competence and capability factors need addressing in a very specific way.

There is a very precise formula for these types of discussion and must, for legal and ethical reasons be tackled with structure and formality. Please seek guidance from a Human Resources expert if there are any doubts about how to tackle a performance issue and what action is needed to manage the discussion appropriately and in line with current legislation.

Handling Put Downs and Criticism

Put downs are where someone takes a passive aggressive stance with us and strips us of our confidence by subtly undermining us or violating our basic human rights. The comments are designed to make us feel uncomfortable, manipulated or intimidated and is intended to make the insecure deliverer feel more powerful in the process.

The comments are derogatory although are often disguised by a jovial delivery, which lulls us into a false sense of security. It's often when we walk away and reflect on the conversation that we realise that we've been insulted.

Self-protective Strategies

The first thing to remember when handling put-downs is that the person delivering it is demonstrating insecurity. When we understand the reason behind someone's interaction, it immediately restores our self-esteem power and puts us back in a stronger position.

Secondly, in our response we are looking to assert our position and protect our right to be treated fairly and equitably. We are also looking to give a clear message that we have more self-worth than to simply accept the put-down and that we will stand up for ourselves. This approach is likely to prevent any future put-downs, as the deliverer will find someone else from which to gain their power.

Here are some ideas about how to respond to this type of interaction:

- Use some stock phrases that will help navigate a way through the put-down. For example,

  'You can't possibly understand – your too young/too old/too inexperienced.' ***'Well it's interesting you should say that…'***

  'That's ridiculously simple, I can't believe you don't get it.' ***'Perhaps you could explain.'***

- Respond with facts where it is appropriate for example:

  'You haven't done the washing yet!' ***'No, not yet.'***

- Ask questions as a way of opening up the interaction and changing its dynamic, for example:

  'What do you mean it's difficult, it's so simple, any fool can see that.' ***'So how would you tackle it then?'***

  You haven't done the washing yet!' ***'No, not yet, when did you need it done by.'***

Handling Stress and Anxiety

Stress is a very real condition in today's modern society and one that we can not ignore. It is the source of many illnesses that manifest themselves phyiscally, mentally and emotionally. The effects are profound and without our knowing, have a deep-rooted impact at a cellular level. It creates tension, dehydration and adrenal pressure as we release the hormone Cortisol to cope with the flight or fight response to a given situation. The label *stress* may well be over-used, although it should not be underestimated at our peril.

Many clients and workshop participants have often asked me whether there is a certain personality type that suffers from stress and anxiety and I believe that this is so. Those of us with a propensity for passive traits will succumbe to stress more often and more naturally because of our need to please and be liked. Accompanying these is the fear that those needs will not be met and hence we feel anxious, which in turn leads to stress.

Stress is made up of excesses, life pressures and physical symptoms, sensations and thoughts, all caused by imbalances in our decision making, either consciously or unconsciously. It is produced through the chemical reaction of our *flight and fight* response and can be really helpful when we are faced with danger or a threat. Our body then returns to its natural state of relaxation.

Unfortunately because our bodies and minds are under so much constant pressure, we have learnt to remain in the *high alert phase* more often than not and this puts undue stress on our organs and our coping mechanisms.

The first step in handling stress is to identify the stress response in our own bodies. Stress affects us all differently and whilst it's my belief that certain personality types may well suffer more than another, stress is a chemical reaction that is in-built and innate – so we all experience it. Look for specific symptoms that are patterns, for example regular headaches, nausia, IBS symptoms, unsettled tummy or shortness of breath.

This is not an exhaustive list, although it's worth tuning into our bodies and noticing what tension, pain or discomfort we experience. This is an important starting point.

Follow this up with an assessment of situations or people that we find stressful and examine what it is about it or them that generates a stress response in us. Once we identify that, using the techniques in this book, we are well on the way to resolving those stressful situations, assertively.

The most important stress reliever is to recognise that relaxation is an active practice and we must instigate it if we are going to create a better balance in our lives. Making a commitment to ourselves that we deserve to return to our natural state of relaxation is paramount to our overall well-being. Here are some activities to engage in that return us to the state that nature intended:

- **Create time and space for ourselves during the day.** Identify a time when we can be alone doing what we enjoy most. That might be as simple has having a relaxing bath or engaging in a sport or hobby that brings us joy and pleasure.

- **Practise the art of mindfulness.** Mindfulness is taking our awareness to a very conscious level, where we can notice every breath, every movement, every thought. Our conscious mind is constantly working, thinking, problem solving and judging, often creating internal turmoil. Retuning our mind and focusing it inwards gives us a stillness and the opportunity to see the world with refreshed eyes.

- **Set aside time to focus on our breathing.** Either through the art of meditation or simply before we go to sleep, allowing our bodies to be still. The breath happens irrespective of our conscious awareness and yet when we can channel and deepen our breathing, it can become healing, restorative and energy giving. Learning to breathe from the belly will calm an over-anxious mind. Breathing from the chest will give us energy if we are feeling lethargic. The breath is life-giving and with great awareness and respect, the breath can begin to return us to the very centre of who we really are.

- **Do one activity each day that brings joy and happiness.** That might be engaged with someone else or alone. The activity will alter our energy vibrations and create a completely different experience of the world.

- **Cook and eat food that is nourishing and in a relaxed way.** Take time to eat, appreciate and digest our food so that our bodies can extract the nutrients it needs to fuel our day to day coping mechanisms. If our bodies are depleted of the essential vitamins and minerals, the effects of our stress will soon take its toil on the inner core of our being.

- **Identify the negativity that we generate ourselves by examining the quality of our thoughts.** Much of our stress is a direct result of our response to a given situation, so we have a choice about the way we react to things. We can choose to be stressed or we can take a step back and consider alternative ways of dealing with stressful events.

- If in the midst of a stressful situation, **create a diversion or distance from the situation** so we can look at the event with objective eyes and not be dragged into old patterns of behaviour. Use the breath to gain control of how we are feeling.

- **Engage in exercise** that either stimulates us aerobically or that gives the immune and nervous system permission to calm and restore. Yoga, Walking, Thai Chi, Pilates are all restorative exercises that nourish and nuture the body back to its natural state. Aerobic exercise can be ideal to burn off excessive tension, although listen to the body and be careful not to over-stretch or do too much. Learn to respect and hear what the body is telling us.

- **Sleep is vital** if we are going to cope with life's stresses and depleted rest is tantamount to disaster. Night time is where our organs restore and without sufficient rest, they are under continual pressure.

Stress is part of our life, although we can choose how we deal with it and the impact it has on our lives. Learning to acknowledge how stress affects us is the first important step to getting control of it and managing a better balance. More importantly, realising that we have a choice is so empowering and realising that we are the masters of our own destiny and not victims to the Matrix.

I hope this collection of difficult situations has been useful and has resonated at some level. Our assertion needs are unique and one person's concerns are another's strength. Acknowledging our capabilities and development areas are so important, enabling us to target our learning specifically rather than generically.

"You don't get harmony when everyone sings the same note."

Doug Floyd

Chapter 4
Assertive Strategy Guide

"Our greatest enemy, the one we must fight most often, is within."

Thomas Paine

This final, technical section provides a useful One-Chapter Guide to all the techniques that I have discussed through the course of the book.

Self-awareness Strategies

The first section focused on self-awareness being the key to developing greater assertion. Using the new paradigm of looking within, we can move beyond the classical *sticking plaster regime* and create authentic change by understanding what makes us behave the way we do. Self-knowledge is absolutely at the heart of our happiness, success and fulfilment. Here is a summary of the self-awareness tools I have shared:

- **Understand our Hilltop.** When we recognise our influences, the people or events that shape us, we can begin to see where our patterns of behaviour come from. This realisation plays an important role in seeing why we do what we do and, therefore, noticing what needs to change. Unconstructive patterns soon impede our success and happiness and understanding the deep-rooted influences that we use as our reference points and decision drivers, are primary steps.

- **Understand our Triggers.** When we have explored the composition of our hilltop, we can then discover more readily what triggers us to think, feel and behave a certain way. Learn to understand that someone or something will subliminally hook us into thinking a certain way, feeling an emotion and ultimately creating an interaction. Knowing our trigger points helps us to uncover why they provoke us and we can begin to unravel the web that surrounds it, thereby creating more constructive responses in our thinking and behaviour.

- **Know our Values, Attitudes and Behaviour patterns.** Invest time in learning what is important to us as this develops an appreciation of the source of our decisions and actions. Values are cornerstones of our behaviour and recognising our core values enables us to choose our responses more wisely and recognise where our internal conflicts come from. Also being able to recognise thinking and behavioural patterns enables us to identify those unhealthier habits that drive unconstructive interactions with our friends, family and work colleagues.

Thinking Strategies

The second part of this book helped us to appreciate the critical role that our mind has on our behaviours. When we recognise the huge influence that our subconscious thoughts have on our self-esteem and that subsequently shape our predominant behaviours, we have the key to transforming our assertion. What we think really does shape what we do. Here is a summary of the mental muscle workouts that we need to engage in.

- **Circles of Influence.** The late Stephen Covey talked about understanding where to put our energy. When we consistently put energy into things that are outside of our control, we cause ourselves stress and frustration. When we focus our energies on what is within our immediate concern, i.e. our behaviours, attitudes and emotions, then we can become more selective in our choices. Actively letting go of situations that are outside of our control or influence, releases more energy for us to invest in other more meaningful and fruitful activities.

- **Look beyond the Front Cover of the Book.** 'Don't judge a book by its cover' is a phrase we are used to hearing and this is so relevant within the assertiveness arena. When we invest in looking, exploring, questioning and understanding, we learn far more than our mere judgements and primal verdicts assume. Enter interactions with the mindset of exploration, compassion and understanding and we will achieve a more meaningful result.

- **Consider other People's Hilltops.** We talked earlier about the importance of looking at our own hilltop. We can also apply the same concept when building an appreciation for other's opinions and behaviours. Think about what might influence someone to think or behave the way they do and that momentary consideration of their world-view instantly creates a stronger compassion and subsequently influence the quality of our interactions.

- **Traffic Light.** Learn to *Stop, Think and Choose.* We instinctively react to events and those interactions end up being less constructive than they could be. When we adopt a pattern of slowing our reactions down, considering our plan and thinking of other's situations, we begin to experience more successful relationships.

- **Get to know SID. S**elf **I**mposed **D**oubts play an invasive role in our self-image. When we explore the SIDs we have dirtying our minds, we begin to challenge their validity by questioning the evidence upon which they are founded. If the evidence is shaky and questionable, then we can learn to dismiss that doubt and replace it with a more constructive thought process.

- **Recalibrate our Thoughts.** When we follow a process of challenging our irrational fears and thoughts, we can begin to retune our repertoire of self-esteem thoughts and craft a new and more constructive internal view. This view becomes the foundation for all our positive thinking and confident behaviour. When we learn to like ourselves, then we can begin to change our interactions with people and stand in our own space with greater strength and character.

- **Learn the Science of Affirmations.** Replacing our old style thinking and creating more affirming beliefs is the source of our change to assertive behaviour. When we think more compassionately about ourselves, we begin to behave more compassionately towards others. Such is the collaboration between thoughts and feelings. If we have little self-respect, we are likely to have little respect for others.

Behavioural Strategies

Woven into each of the three sections has been a kaleidoscope of options that enable us to select more constructive responses. Here is a summary of some of the key elements that I have shared.

- **Let Go of the Apple.** I shared the lovely Buddhist story of the hunter's cunning trick of capturing monkeys by using an enticing apple held in a jar. This tale illustrates the ease at which we attach ourselves to inappropriate events or concerns, stripping us of our energy. When we hold onto things that are not important, our assertiveness suffers. Learn to let go.

- **Broken Record Technique.** This communication strategy encourages us to use the same refusal phrase to demonstrate a strength of opinion to a given situation. Rather than sounding indecisive with a range of different excuses, the broken record shows tenacity.

- **Tranformational Interactions.** Develop engaging, involving and meaningful conversations by putting others at the forefront of our minds. When we communicate with meaning and purpose, our conversations are so much clearer and action oriented.

- **Learn the Art of NLP.** Neuro Linguist Programming is the art of speaking mindfully. Using specific techniques of mirroring, matching and sensory-based language we can engage with people at a much more profound level.

- **Be Fascinated by People.** When we put people at the heart of our relationships, we develop more meaningful conversations that are empathic and compassionate. When we invest in listening, understanding and observing, our approach becomes based on respect, which is at the heart of any assertive strategy.

- **Ask more Questions.** Questioning is an important art if we want to succeed and fulfil our potential. Open questions are the key to opening up conversations and exploring the root-cause of a situation or issue.

- **Be Outcome-focused.** The clearer we are on what we hope to achieve from an interaction or event, the more successful the result. People need structure, clarity and direction and so in our assertive development we can provide these by being clear in our own minds.

- **Fogging.** When involved in a conflict or confrontation, learn to use the fogging technique that initially demonstrates an agreement with the protagonist, before then adding the assertion phrase. This element of surprise unstablises them and creates an opening for discussion.

- **Use the Appreciation Frame.** During a conflict, the use of the Appreciation Frame can come in very handy. Be careful not to follow the chosen verb with BUT or HOWEVER as these negate the sentiment of the phrase. The options are:

  - I agree
  - I understand
  - I appreciate.

Not every strategy listed here will suit each situation we are faced with. We must apply the discipline of considering the most appropriate approach if we are going to succeed in our assertion.

Through practise we soon learn which of these strategies deliver the best and most collaborative result. Over the coming weeks/months, experiment with these techniques and review the success of each interaction, adapting the approach each time. The more we apply, learn and alter our interactions, the more comfortable we become.

Summary of Assertive Skills

Finally, here is a list of all the subtleties that lie within the assertive spectrum that open the door to a more positive outcome.

• Express what you are thinking	• Take the initiative
• Breathe when anxious	• Use the Appreciation Frame
• Ask for clarification	• Aim for collaboration
• Solve problems with people	• Timing is everything
• Adopt new internal dialogue	• Think before speaking
• Use open questions and listen	• Use positive communication
• Hold eye contact and smile	• Take responsibility
• Choose behaviour according to the person and the situation	• Be sensitive to and respect ours and other's feelings
• Reframe negative inner dialogue	• Deal with behaviour not personalities
• Learn to compromise rather than say 'No'	• Discuss options in conflict
• Focus on others when communicating	• Be factual
• Let go of negative beliefs	• Avoid making judgements
• Use personal references:	• Avoid exaggerations such as:

• This is the way I see it • In my opinion • This is how I feel • This is what it means to me	• You are **never** on time • You **always** leave your shirts on the floor • You **never** listen to me

• Understand other's points of view and acknowledge others more.	• Use a formula such as:
	
	  • I feel (state your feeling)
	
	  • When (describe the behaviour)
	
	  • Because (concrete effect)
	
	  • I'd prefer it if (offer compromise)

"He who desires but acts not, breeds pestilence."

Bacon

Chapter 5
Action Planning

"In everything, the ends well defined, are the secret of durable success."

Victor Cousins, Philosopher

Many books we read, especially in the 'self-help' genre uplift us, perhaps even motivate us, although if they don't inspire action and change, then the reading investment may be thwarted.

Change comes about when we are inspired to take action to doing, thinking or feeling differently. Although we must be proactive, and courageous otherwise we maintain a status quo.

As we saw in the first section of this book, committing to some action planning is essential to the creation and sustaining of change. And so in the spirit of transparency and clarity, I have chosen to repeat the steps and process in detail that I outlined in Part 1.

Having read this whole book, what do you feel determined to change, inspired to do differently? Thinking these questions through is so important if you really want to revel in the positive results awaiting you.

As with the previous two sections, the action planning is important as we begin to make commitments to our future and the change that we feel inspired to instigate. For transparency, the same six steps, hold the key for our transformational expansion

Six Steps to Making Change Happen

Step 1 – Review your Learning

Reflecting back on the exercises, think about what stood out, resonated or meant something. There has been plenty to contemplate, so collecting your thoughts and gathering up what have been the most useful discoveries is an important step before you begin translating those into goals.

Learning Review Exercise

Return to each chapter, noting down the elements that have struck a chord with you.

Then go back to chapter 1, where I asked you to consider your assertive vision and based on that information, record what have you learned and discovered.

Step 2 – Review your Goals

As you review your vision, you may feel that it needs reworking or that it is too woolly, especially given your discoveries. This is natural. Visions and goals need to be flexible and adaptive, so use them as a reference point. If you believe your vision needs to change, carry on to the Goal Review exercise below, otherwise move on to Step 3.

Goal Review Exercise

If your vision needs to change, rewrite what you want to achieve based on your learning. Consider what you want to look, sound and feel like one year from now.

With your vision revised, you can now return to your learning review notes and identify which discoveries most help you achieve that vision over the coming year.

Step 3 – Your Inspirations

When we are really inspired to do something, nothing stops us. Think back to a time when you have had a real passion, an energy to do, say a marathon, prepare for an interview or work for a charity that is close to your heart. Even though you are busy, you make time for inspirational activities.

Inspirations Exercise

Albert Einstein said, *'Genius is 1% inspiration and 99% perspiration'.* This may be true, although if we don't have inspiration in the first place, then our perspiration is wasted sweat.

List what you feel most inspired to do differently that will help you towards your newly revised goals in Chapter 1. Only list three things so that you keep focused.

Step 4 – Questions are the Answers

Throughout the book I have discussed the importance of questions and now it is time to employ that skill in setting your action plan. Taking the three most relevant inspirations that have had the greatest impact on you, formulate each one into a measurable and tangible action using the following six questions:

What: will you specifically do differently?

Why: is this action important to you?

How: will you approach achieving this action?

When: will you do this, over what period?

Who: will need to support you and who is involved?

Where: will this goal take place? Be specific.

This now gives your actions structure and helps them become meaningful statements of intent.

Step 5 – Do and Review

> *"We are what we repeatedly do. Excellence then, is not an act, but a habit."*

Aristotle

It is now time to take action and repeated action at that. Inspired by your commitments, you need to go forth and apply yourself. To help you, here is some guidance about making it a long-lasting change and not just a 'five minute wonder'.

- **Focus only on three commitments.** If you adopt any more it will become like a shopping list, often overwhelming and soon forgotten. When you have changed those commitments into new habits, then you can identify your next set of actions.

- **Repeat your actions regularly.** The more you repeat, the more you hone and gain in confidence. After all, *'Repetition is the Mother of skill.'*

- **Involve people in your changes.** Talk to people close to you about your changes, especially family and friends. With their inclusion, you secure their support rather than create fear, suspicion or threat.

- **Carry out regular reviews and document your successes.** The more you assess your progress and celebrate what is going well, the more momentum you will experience. You will also be more in tune with what is working less well and be able to make adjustments.

- **Celebrate your successes.** It is important to acknowledge what is going well. Share those successes with friends who will be interested or your partner. The act of sharing itself reinforces the positivity of the action and inspires you to continue.

Step 6 – Commit to Paper

Remember that it's proven when we write down our goals, we are more likely to stick to them. So I encourage you to commit your intentions to paper and make them public where you will see them regularly.

With knowledge, confidence, self-assuredness and a handful of tools to use in your most challenging situations, you are now ready to forge ahead and create a new future – full of possibilities, fulfilment and well-being.

Once again, I encourage you to use the next **four to six weeks** to experiment, talk, journalise and reflect on what is going well and what still needs adjusting. Change rarely comes over night, although it will be a swift as you believe it can be.

Mastering assertion is a true journey – one that never really ends. Like every path, there may seem to be a destination, although there is always another fork we can take and sometimes that might mean treading in the same footprints as before. I encourage you to revisit this book and allow the concepts, guidance and learning to embed in your mind. The more you want this, the more it will become a way of life.

I have enjoyed travelling with you along the way and I genuinely hope that your discoveries only serve to excite you about the possibilities that self-knowledge, power of the mind and mindful behaviours can offer your life. I wish you success, fulfilment and happiness in all you do.

"When we open our eyes to the infinite possibilities, we realise how much we could be, have and do. It's time to make it so.

Karen Davies, Coach

References/Resources

Feel the Fear and Do It Anyway	Susan Jeffers
Take Time for Your Life	Cheryl Richardson
Assert Yourself	Gael Lindenfield
How to Develop Assertiveness	Sam R Lloyd
Know Yourself	Ellen Balke
Awaken the Giant Within	Anthony Robbins
Seven Habits of Highly Effective People	Stephen Covey
Creating Self-esteem	Lynda Field
The Biology of Belief	Bruce Lipton
You Can Have What You Want	Michael Neill
You Can Heal Your Own Life	Louise Hay
It's the Thought that Counts	David R. Hamilton
How your Mind Can Heal your Body	David R. Hamilton
Life Changing Magic	Michael Kewley
The Power of the Subconscious Mind	Joseph Murphy
Mindsight	Dr Daniel Siegel
Assert Yourself	Gael Lindenfield
How to develop Assertiveness	Sam R Lloyd
Free Yourself From Harmful Stress	Trevor Powell
www.briantracy.com	Official website
www.christianpankhurst.com	Official website

Printed in Poland
by Amazon Fulfillment
Poland Sp. z o.o., Wrocław